# An Investigation into the Economic Determinants of Fertility

# American University Studies

Series XVI
Economics

Vol. 1

PETER LANG
New York · Berne · Frankfort on the Main · Nancy

Robert Allen Kohl

# An Investigation in the Economic Determinants of Fertility

PETER LANG
New York · Berne · Frankfort on the Main · Nancy

CIP-Kurztitelaufnahme der Deutschen Bibliothek

**Kohl, Robert Allen:**
An investigation into the economic determinants
of fertility / Robert Allen Kohl. – New York;
Berne; Frankfort on the Main; Nancy: Lang, 1984.
   (American University Studies: Ser. 16, Economics;
   Vol. 1)
   ISBN 0-8204-0086-6

NE: American University Studies / 16


Library of Congress Cataloging in Publication Data

**Kohl, Robert Allen, 1947–**
   An investigation into the economic determinants of
fertility.
   (American University Studies. Series XVI, Economics,
ISSN 0741-2150; v. 1)
   Bibliography: p.
   1. Fertility, Human – Economic aspects – Mathematical
models.   2. Family size – Economic aspects – Mathematical
models.   I. Title.   II. Series.
HB901.K65   1984        304.6'32'0724        83-49222
ISBN 0-8204-0086-6

© Peter Lang Publishing Inc., New York 1984

Printed by Lang Druck Inc., Liebefeld/Berne (Switzerland)

# TABLE OF CONTENTS

# AN INVESTIGATION INTO
## THE ECONOMIC DETERMINANTS OF FERTILITY

### 1. INTRODUCTION

In recent years, much attention has been given to the possible relationship between economic variables and household fertility behavior. It is my desire to explore the work that has been done to date in this area, and then to develop a model of my own that serves to tie off some of the loose ends which still exist. This problem is of significance, not only from the detached standpoint of academic analysis, but also from the practical perspective of the policy maker. Specifically, various institutions (i.e., public education, social insurance, capital projects whose benefit to cost ratios depend on an accurate anticipation of population growth, etc.) are predicated on the development of a good working model for the prediction of various demographic values. It is my objective, then, to contribute to the formulation of such a model.

### ECONOMIC CALCULUS AND FERTILITY BEHAVIOR

With the notable exception of Malthus, students of economic relationships have until quite recently shown little interest in the construction of models in which fertility behavior is made to depend on economic factors. Indeed, curiosity about the economic consequences of exogenously determined demographic conditions is, again with the exception of Malthus, confined as well to recent decades of the twentieth century. Since this point is discussed at greater

length in Chapter 2, it is sufficient to say here that the
economics discipline, adopting the course charted by Smith
and Ricardo, has sought to confine itself to a temporal context for which the positive sum outcome associated with free
exchange is stable. The reason for this rejection of the
Malthusean alternative (i.e., that population growth ultimately renders 'prosperity' an unstable state) appears, I
believe, to rest on two supporting ideas. First, both superficial and detailed observations have led us to conclude
that a state in which the living standard is above mean subsistance can indeed enjoy a measure of stability. Thus, if
a correlation does exist between family size and family income, it is one whose significance is trivial, except perhaps in the very long run. Secondly, orthodox economic
thought has tended to confine itself to the relationship between social man and the material world. The emphasis placed
on the term 'scarcity' in any principles text, or the rele-
gation of individual idiosyncracies within consumer demand or
factor supply models to a status of miscellaneous 'tastes and
preferences', elements of which follow standardized normal
distributions having zero covariances with income and price
variables, both seem to drive this point home. If then, fertility has proved itself to be empirically insensitive to
economic factors, it follows that economists would tend to
eschew its employment, certainly as a dependent variable,
leaving that task to demographers, biologists, and perhaps

sociologists. Betraying a measure of disciplinary prejudice similar to that of economists, the latter have in many cases elevated our 'tastes and preferences' to such a degree that numerous specific and often interdependent factors, or 'norms', have been identified. At the same time, however, the many and diverse price and income variables of key interest to economists are themselves combined into a single category, i.e., income per capita, or calories produced per person per year.

First in the 1930's, and then in the 1950's and subsequently, renewed interest by economists in fertility has taken place, although ironically, this renaissance of the Malthusean course was brought about by observations which, if anything, appear to stand Malthus on his head. Specifically, the phenomenon of demographic transition has led us to suspect once again that material factors may indeed play a significant role in intended family size. What surprises us, however, is that these factors appear to have moved in such a way as to lead many scholars to the conclusion that there is a negative secular correlation between that single representative of economic conditions (i.e., income or calories), and fertility. Now, as all economists know, income and fertility cannot be negatively correlated unless the 'services' which parents derive from children are inferior goods. Since the latter are an exception, however, we are generally happier to discover some alternative route of explanation. We conclude, therefore, that secular increases in income per capita must be the 'tip

of an iceberg', the bulk of whose subsurface mass consists of a
wide range of price variables, secular changes for which occur
not only in some regular relationship to long-run swings in
income per capita, but also for which a host of anti-fertility
substitution effects are associated. To illustrate, protracted economic development leads to an increase in the need for
urban labor relative to rural labor, the demands for urban products being income elastic relative to those of rural products.
Because urban production tends to be the more contralized, however, that parent (usually the wife) who could previously provide child rearing as well as other productive services simultaneously, now finds herself forced to choose between the home
or the labor market. Thus, as further development stimulates
labor market demand for her time, the opportunity cost of rearing children grows. Ergo, the negative secular correlation
between income and fertility is spurious since it is the substitution effect from a change in the value of wife's time,
and not higher incomes, that accounts for smaller families.

In a sense, one could say that economists, long having ignored Malthus, are coming to his rescue, at least so far as
the normal good status of child services is concerned. The
literature discussed in the next two chapters testifies to
this. Easterlin, a pioneer in the attempt to identify the
economic determinants of fertility behavior, puts forth an
effort (1967) to explain the reduction in fertility rates in
the U.S. from their 1957 peak, despite continued brisk growth

in income per capita, as a phenomenon that would have been substantially more precipitous had continued prosperity not occured. Using Easterlin's methodology, several students had varying degrees of success during the mid and late 1960's in showing that the inclusion within a regression model designed to predict fertility of a sufficient number of relevant independent variables, in addition to income, usually reveals a coefficient for the latter that is positive and (frequently) significant. Absent from this work, however, is the kind of rigorous theoretical basis that most economists have come to expect. Here, the pathbreaking efforts of Becker and his associates at Chicago have, I believe, gone a long way to plug this gap, indicating both theoretically and empirically that the positive pure income effect on the demand for numbers of children is the rule rather than the exception. Although there appear to be reversals here, the Becker approach clearly implies that they are, in reality, the result of special substitution effects arising from the interaction between numbers and quality of children.

Since I intend to construct my own model of fertility behavior along the theoretical guidelines set down by Becker, et al, I believe it necessary to point out that this most recent approach has not been entirely free from criticism. In the first place, there is a question of propriety. In addressing this issue, T.W. Schultz suggests:

"I anticipate that many sensitive, thoughtful
people will be offended by these studies of fertility because they may see them as debasing the
family and motherhood."[1]

Schultz goes on to refute the charge that the materially

oriented economic calculus is making inappropriate invasion

into the sanctity of the family by pointing out that at

least part of the decision of family size is indeed of a ma-

terial nature. Specifically, children are, and have tradi-

tionally been, of tangible value as items of human capital,

the latter being a subject area in which Schultz has been

especially active. Thus, while it may give us cause for dis-

may, the fact remains that children require an investment of

material inputs, and that at the margin, their potential

ability to compensate for these costs quite frequently deter-

mines whether or not parents choose to have one more of them.

I believe our critics are on somewhat firmer ground when

they suggest that these recent developments are incorrect in

their adoption of the techniques of constrained maximization

as a theoretical point of departure. In short, most of these

models, including my own (Chapter 4), seem to suggest that

(a) a single utility function exists for parents, and (b)

children are little more than arguments within this function.

Thus, the possibility that a distinct utility function for

each child exists, and will, with the appearance of that child,

---

[1]T.W. Schultz, "The Value of Children: An Economic Perspective." JOURNAL OF POLITICAL ECONOMY (Vol. 81,
Number 2, Part II, March/April, 1973),
pp. S2-3.

cause the form of the parents' function(s) to be altered seems to be ignored. Commenting on a contribution made along these lines by Willis (1973), Ryder, while offering support to these efforts to introduce economic analysis to family planning, warns that there are dangers associated with an approach that appears to ignore the very real presence of altruism within the family.

While one welcomes Ryder's support, and recognizes the validity of his criticism, it must be pointed out that this caveat is not new. Indeed, a necessary condition for the existence of a Bergson-Samuelson 'family welfare function' is that the utility functions of individual family members be independent. Acknowledging this, Willis does reflect on Samuelson's admission that "Where the family is concerned, the phenomenon of altruism inevitably raises its head..."[2]

"Samuelson's emphasis can be reversed, however. The family exists as an institution because, given altruism and the nonmarket mechanisms by which it is able to allocate commodities and welfare among its members, it has both the incentive and the capacity to resolve allocative problems involving public goods, externalities, and the like that in impersonal markets inevitably lead to market imperfections. The capacity of the family to resolve these problems efficiently provides a basis for a positive theory of family behavior, because, given efficient allocation, the family will tend to respond systematically to changes in the position or shape of the constraints it faces..."[3]

[2]P.A. Samuelson, "Social Indifference Curves", QUARTERLY JOURNAL OF ECONOMICS 70(Feb., 1956) p. 9.

[3]R.J. Willis, "A New Approach to the Economic Theory of Fertility Behavior", JOURNAL OF POLITICAL ECONOMY (vo. cit.) p. S19.

Taking prudent recognition of the warnings of those both within and outside the economics profession, we admit the implications these warnings have concerning how far we can go. With the firm belief, however, that that distance is at least sufficient to justify the necessary efforts, we may proceed.

AGENDA

It is my principal objective to examine the roles played by income and various socioeconomic factors in household fertility planning. I begin by constructing a model along those lines suggested by Becker. Specifically, children and alternatives to children are produced at home with inputs of parents' time and market goods. Operating under the assumption that the production of child services is the more time intensive, then, testable hypotheses about substitution and income effects associated with changes in independent variables can be deduced.

While my interest is focused for the most part on the microeconomic aspects of family planning, I believe it wise not to lose sight of the larger question of economic development and population growth. With this in mind, Chapter 2 contains a brief examination of the two alternative perspectives on this question, i.e., the anti-natalist position of Coale & Hoover, and Enke, as well as the pro-natalist perspective of Kuznets and J. Simon. This is followed by a discussion of some early work done by those who would make fertility the dependent variable. Here, I focus on some of

Leibenstein's observations, Easterlin's analysis of the post
World War II 'baby boom' in the U.S., and finally, on those
attempts in the mid 1960's to use regression analysis to
identify factors other than income which may play a key role
in determining family size.

A summary of Becker's theoretical work is presented in
Chapter 3. Here, I concentrate most of my attention on the
theory of the allocation of time (Becker--1965), although some
measure of depth is provided via an examination of the interaction between quantity and quality of offspring (Becker--
1960, 1973, 1981). In addition, some recent modifications
made by T.P. Schultz (1969), Willis (1973), and Michael (1973)
in such areas as the effects of child mortality, the theoretical differentiation between the behavior of working as opposed
to non-working wives, and parents' education are also discussed. Finally, I examine some of the attempts to expose
Becker's theoretical framework to econometric testing. Here,
efforts by T.P. Schultz (1969), Willis (1973), DeTray (1973),
Gardner (1973), Cain & Dooley (1976), and Fleisher & Rhodes
(1979) are noted.

The theoretical basis for my own model is presented in
Chapter 4. In the spirit of Becker et al, I begin with a
household welfare function whose arguments are Numbers of
Children, Child Premium, and Living Standard. While each of
these items is produced in the home using inputs of market
goods and time, it is assumed that the husband is the primary

source of labor market income, and that while his home time may be substituted for that of the wife, total time required for household production will be at least as great as what he can provide himself. It is also assumed that the production function for numbers of children, while possibly subject to economies of scale, implies, more importantly, that child rearing is more time intensive than is the consumption of alternatives to children.

My own concept of 'Child Premium' differs in two ways from the 'Child Quality' used by Becker and others. First, while the latter is confined to investment in such items as the future earning ability or life expectancy of offspring, child premium goes a step further, including those inputs of time and goods contributed by parents in order to derive certain intangible kinds of satisfaction from children. In view of this first distinction, a second digression from Becker's concept of quality involves my decision to incorporate the interaction between quantity and quality into the framework of the utility function, rather than that of the constraint of the maximization problem, the latter being the usual procedure found in the post-Becker literature.

Maximization of utility (or family welfare) is of course constrained by the household production functions, and ultimately, wife's available time, her market wage rate, and husband's and external sources of income. It is assumed that a strategy for maximizing family welfare subject to these con-

straints is made in an atmosphere of perfect certainty (or
at least perfect knowledge of probabilities of events that
could alter this strategy) by parents at the time of household formation.

After determining the signs of substitution and income
effects resulting from changes in wife's wage or husband's
(or external) income, I proceed to make what I consider to be
my initial contribution to the understanding of these aspects
of fertility behavior. Specifically, by suggesting how such
socioeconomic factors as grandparents' income (a proxy for
status), parents' education, and urbanization can be woven
into the fabric of the constrained maximization problem, it can
be shown that changes in any of these could also generate traditional substitution and/or income effects, or, what I choose
to call 'utility substitution effects'. There are also possibilities of 'risk effects' should provision be made for stochastic factors such as infant mortality or contraceptive
strategy. Thus, the essentially short-run character of Becker's original procedure can be generalized into a long-run
economic model of fertility behavior.

Initial tests of the model are presented in Chapter 5.
Here, I believe the main contribution to be the establishment
of a 'temporal framework' in which each socioeconomic or income variable is arranged on one of several 'levels of causality'. In this way, I believe I can provide a method for
dealing with multicollinearity by paying heed to the causal

subservience of some independent variables to others.

By way of procedure, I employ corss-sectional data (1970 Census of Population) selected from each of three regions of the United States. Specifically, samples of approximately 200 counties are drawn from the Midwest (i.e., Iowa, Kansas, and Nebraska), the Northeast (New York, Ohio, and Pennsylvania), and the Southeast (Alabama and Georgia). Since sample means vary with respect to both the dependent and the independent variables, seperate sets of regressions for each region permit me to compare coefficients with regional means. I may thus determine (a) likely areas of interaction among independent variables, (b) possible biases associated with proxies used, and (c) general behavioral differences among the three regions.

The results obtained are quite interesting. First, I find that the model is much more successful in accounting for variance in family size in the Southeast than in the other two regions. Since mean values of income variables are somewhat lower in the Southeast than elsewhere, there seems to be a strong suggestion that in a region that is less developed economically, socioeconomic factors play a more profound role in family planning. A second major observation deals with the proxies for husband's income and wife's wage. Specifically, the latter are quite close to each other for the Midwest and Northeast. For the Southeast, however, the algebraic value of the wife's wage coefficient is substantially less than that of the coefficient of husband's income. This observation is interesting because it implies that, with economic development as reflected in family income, there is also a reduction in the time intensity of child rearing relative to that of consuming alternatives to children. Finally, coefficients of the status variable (i.e., grandparents' income) reveal the presence of a very strong negative utility substitution effect in the Southeast, i.e., that region for which mean family size is greatest; and virtually no utility substitution effect in the Northeast, i.e., where mean fertility is least. In short, it appears that differences in parents' financial backgrounds before marriage tend, with economic development, to diminish in importance as a determining factor in fertility behavior.

Since the mid 1970's, the Becker approach to fertility behavior appears to have divided into two lines of investigation. One course involves the development of models designed to predict the distribution of such activities as child rearing and wife's labor market participation throughout the family life cycle. While there is much to be learned here, I have decided to pursue in Chapter 6 the alternative direction of interest, that is, the development and testing of a model designed to explain the determinants of wife's wage, wife's labor supply, and the demands for numbers of children and child premium simultaneously.

Concerning fertility behavior, the regressions designed to examine the more complete model leave intact those observations made in Chapter 5. Indeed, the conclusion that socio-

economic factors play a key role in family decisions in economically less developed regions is reenforced by the ability
of proxies for housing demand and wife's labor supply to explain for the Southeast region a significant proportion of
the variance in numbers of children not accounted for in the
model in which those independent factors were absent.

With respect to regressions testing housing demand and
wife's labor force participation, coefficient signs appear to
be consistent for all three regions with those obtained in
regressions measuring fertility behavior. For example, the
coefficient of grandparents' income is strongly positive in
the Southeast regression for housing demand. This reflects a
positive utility substitution effect favoring alternatives to
children that complements the negative utility substitution
effect which status was found to have on the demand for child
services per se. In contrast, this coefficient is not significant for Northeastern and Midwestern regressions, just as
previous living standard was similarly of no significance in
fertility regressions for the latter two regions. In the case
of wife's labor supply, the coefficient of family size is negative and quite significant in the Southeastern regression,
underscoring the apparent time intensity of child rearing in
the economically least developed region. In the Northeast
and Midwest, where 'child service production' appears to require a relatively lower input of wife's time, I find her labor force behavior to be minimally affected by the presence of

children.

Having discussed these and other observations directly
related to my empirical findings, I am ready to set down a
number of general conclusions, and to offer suggestions for
possible courses of future research. These tasks are performed in Chapter 7.

## 2. FERTILITY AND ECONOMIC DEVELOPMENT:
### THE SETTING

Before concentrating on the principal issue at hand, that
is, the economic determinants of long-run fertility behavior,
valuable insights can be gained by a brief review of some of
the pioneering perspectives on the larger issue of the interdependence of population growth and economic development.
Upon inspection of the literature, two themes appear to present
themselves. First, attitudes seem to have come full circle
since the initial inquiries of Malthus. Specifically, the
Essay on Population (1798) gives fertility prime consideration
as an endogenous variable, simultaneously determining and being determined by 'subsistance' per capita. From that time,
however, until the 1930's, the general attitude of economists
has been to concentrate on the 'short run', i.e., that temporal context in which population growth is either ignored
completely, or at best, relegated to the status of a purely
exogenous factor. Since the thirties, renewed interest has
occured. First with stagnation theories, and later with the
emergence of Neo-Malthuseans and their opponents, once again,
economists have employed the unique tools of their discipline
for the examination of this issue. This brings us to a second
theme. Specifically, if we are going to admit fertility behavior as an endogenous factor within our models of growth and
fluctuations, should this variable be considered dependent,
independent, or co-dependent? Clearly, this question is rhe-
torical since most students of fertility behavior would, in
the spirit of Malthus, agree to the proposition that there is

an interdependence between the forces that affect productivity and the forces that affect fertility. Indeed, this interdependence is at the crux of Malthus' model. Still, we observe that there have been at the least several changes in perspective since the rebirth of interest during the thirties. Looking at fertility as an independent variable, we find very important contributions made by, and indeed still being made by Kuznets, Coale & Hoover, Enke, J. Simon, and others. Of course, the alternative viewpoint, though perhaps more recent in the literature, is also well represented, first by Leibenstein and Easterlin, and more recently by Becker and his associates.

While the bulk of my own efforts are consistent with this latter approach, it must be stated that there is much to be learned from a study of both directions of causality. For this reason, I present in this chapter a review of some of the ideas of those who have focused on fertility as the independent variable. That having been done, the chapter concludes with a discussion of the pre-Becker efforts made by Leibenstein and Easterlin to view desired family size as a function of economic variables.

FROM MALTHUS TO DEMOGRAPHIC TRANSITION

To begin, I review the Malthusean model of population growth and productivity change, and then by way of contrast, the model of demographic transition.

Malthus: As we are all aware, the initial attempt to

draw a relationship between population growth and economic factors was made by Thomas Malthus in his ESSAY ON POPULATION. Here, Malthus constructs a model in which population will always tend toward some equilibrium level. This conclusion follows from two basic assumptions: (a) Technology: As more labor is combined with a finite amount of land, output rises at a declining rate, so that at some point, output per worker begins to decline, and (b) Behavior: Mortality varies inversely and fertility varies directly with output per capita. Given that the size of the labor force is some exogenously determined and stable proportion of the population, then, it follows that a state of prosperity (i.e., output per capita greater than that value for which fertility equals mortality) contains the seeds of its own demise. Of interest here is the positive correlation assumed to exist between output per capita and fertility. While this relationship seems to hold true over short periods of time, the experience of economically developed societies has been one of long-run, or secular declines in fertility co-existing with long-run advances in living standard.

Demographic Transition: This latter observation has provided the basis for an alternative to the Malthusean approach, beginning first with the work of demographers such as Blacker, Thompson, Landry, Notestein, and others.[1] While each of these individuals presents a unique model, there are certain key as-

---

[1]See: H. Leibenstein, ECONOMIC BACKWARDNESS AND ECONOMIC GROWTH, New York, John Wiley & Sons, 1957, p. 155

pects which all have in common. Specifically, as a society is transformed from a less into a more developed economic entity, the initial demographic effect is a sharp fall in mortality rates. The resulting gap between still high birth rates and these reduced numbers of deaths is thus responsible for the rapid growth of population typical of Western Europe and North America during the Nineteenth Century, and of Japan more recently. After a lag of perhaps a generation, however, birth rates follow mortality rates in a downward direction. Consequently, a new equilibrium is achieved with development accounting for lower rates of birth, mortality, and subsequently, population growth.

The principal question then involves whether or not those factors accounting for the completion of the transition (i.e., lower birth rates) in currently developed countries can be depended on to have the same effect in currently less developed societies, where the first phase of the transition (i.e., lower mortality) has already happened.[2]

As noted, the transition model just outlined is given to us by demographers. It is disturbing to economists because it is in apparent contradiction to the predictions offered by the only model of population growth provided by our discipline through the first third of this century, i.e., that of Malthus. It has behooved us, therefore, to construct an alternative model for which these observations are in conformity.

[2]Recent data suggest that, indeed, most middle income and even several LDC's are experiencing declining fertility rates. See: World Bank, WORLD DEVELOPMENT REPORT 1981, New York, Oxford University Press, 1981, Table 18, p. 169.

FERTILITY AS THE INDEPENDENT VARIABLE

In this section, I examine some of the more noteworthy
attempts to treat economic development, i.e., a sustained rise
in income per capita, as a phenomenon dependent on long-run
fertility rates. Specifically, given that the decline in mortality is only peripherally related to increased productivity,
especially today when MDC's are able to share the fruits of
medical and public health technology, will the probability of
success at economic development be enhanced or retarded by an
extension of the time lag observed to occur between the fall in
mortality and the eventual decline in fertility? Taking the
'anti-natalist' position that a society's chances of economic
success are improved by a quickening in the adjustment of fertility are Coale & Hoover (1958) and Enke (1970). Defending
the opposite perspective is J. Simon (1977), whose model is designed to incorporate earlier observations made by Kuznets
(1960).[3]

Pro- and Anti-Natalist Positions: In contrasting the models offered by anti-natalists Coale & Hoover, and Enke with
those of pro-natalists Kuznets and Simon, it is useful to examine first the points of similarity. For example, both assume
a single entity economy for which total output follows a Cobb-
Douglas production function. Given specifications governing
such items as the rates of capital formation, labor force
growth, and technological progress, simulations are conducted

[3]See: J. Simon, THE ECONOMICS OF POPULATION GROWTH, Princeton,
N.J., Princeton University Press, 1977, Chapter 6.

using alternative, exogenously determined rates of population growth. Conclusions can then be drawn about the advantages and/or disadvantages of population growth by observing resulting paths of output per capita (Coale & Hoover, Enke) or output per worker (Simon) through time.

Given the similarities between pro- and anti-natalist models, three areas of difference can now be exposed. First, the anti-natalists propose that the rate of net capital formation (s) be a function of both output per capita (q), and the rate of population growth (p), i.e.,

$$(K_t - K_{t-1})/K_{t-1} = s(q,p)$$

In contrast, Simon suggests that 's' be a function of 'p' alone. This is a minor difference, however, since it affects only the timing of Simon's conclusions, and not the conclusions per se.

Secondly, a disagreement exists regarding the appropriate time horizon of such models. Specifically, the anti-natalists confine their simulations to a period of at most thirty years. Thus, a constant labor force (L) is stipulated under the rather obvious assumptions that (a) the rate of labor force participation among adults is constant, and (b) a significant time lag is needed for new members of the population to enter the labor force. As might be suspected, the pro-natalists are skeptical of the utility of this sort of short-run perspective. As Simon notes:

"...it will seldom be meaningful to view a model in the isolation of a short period. And the long run is obviously not simply a series of short-run models strung end to end, at least when assessing the economics of population growth. Hence, for almost all purposes the monetized-capital-effects models of the Coale-Hoover type should be considered too partial for long-run assessment, but rather as useful for yielding crucial inputs to more general models."[4]

Thus, the pro-natalist models express the labor force in time period 't' (i.e., $L_t$) as some proportion of population in time period 't-m', where 'm' represents the number of periods needed for new individuals to attain an appropriate age for labor force participation.

A final, and perhaps the central, point of difference dividing pro- and anti-natalists deals with the technology constant of the aggregate production function (A). Here, the Coale-Hoover and Enke models specify a constant and exogenously determined rate of technological growth (k), i.e.,

$$A_t = A_o e^{kt}$$

This way of treating technology contrasts sharply with that of Kuznets and Simon. According to the latter, 'A' is a "complex of natural resources, economies of scale, and technological knowledge..."[5], and as such, should grow at a rate that is determined endogenously. Specifically, Simon expresses 'k' as a linear function of the labor force size lagged by five years, i.e.,

$$k = bL_{t-5}$$

[4] J. Simon, op cit, p. 237.

[5] ibid., p. 112.

...where 'b' is positive, reflecting Kuznets' observation that
a larger labor force increases the likelihood of technological improvements taking place.[6] Now, when this specification
is incorporated into the simulation process, one finds that
the 'capital diluting' aspects of population growth as indicated by anti-natalist models are eventually overcome by the
growth of technology. Specifically, by assigning values to
'b' that are consistent with those obtained from earlier studies of the components of growth, Simon determines the period
needed to overtake capital dilution to be quite reasonable,
i.e., thirty to fifty years. Moreover, as the rate of population growth increases, so too does the likelihood that the latter range can be shortened.[7]

The Kuznets-Simon approach to the investigation of the
effects of fertility on economic development is an interesting
alternative to that of the anti-natalists. Two reservations
must nevertheless be stated. In the first place, it is a formidable task to seperate econometrically the various elements
of technological growth; not only because many of the aspects
of these elements are non-quantifiable, but also because,
quite frequently, these elements may be overlapping. While
this in itself does not disqualify the basic premise that contributions to knowledge can overcome the effects of capital
dilution, we are also led to wonder (a) if a signifacant portion of Simon's 'b' would remain after a possible exhaustion

[6]ibid., p. 113.

[7]ibid., Table 6-1b, p. 129.

of scale economies, and (b) if the growth of knowledge is
itself especially sensitive to labor force growth. With respect to the latter point, we would be ill advised to ignore
the observations of Schumpeter and others. A second and perhaps more important point, given our present purposes, deals
with the very real possibility that fertility itself is dependent in many ways on economic conditions (and not just vice
versa). Here, two obvious scenarios present themselves.
First, an improvement in economic conditions could stimulate
increased fertility, implying (should the Kuznets-Simon hypothesis be accepted) that growth is explosive. More likely,
however, secular increases in output per capita cause fertility to fall, thus generating the 'S' shaped growth paths
observed in data for currently developed economies.

FERTILITY AS THE DEPENDENT VARIABLE

As stated earlier, those largely responsible for the rebirth among economists of interest in fertility behavior were
individuals primarily concerned with the rôle of population
growth as an independent variable. In this section, I examine
two attempts to consider family size from the alternative perspective.

Leibenstein and the Costs and Utilities of Additional
Children: In 1957, Leibenstein[8], studying the question of economic development, proposed a model designed to explain the
decline in fertility within demographic transition in terms of
economic phenomena. Specifically, children provide parents
[8]Leibenstein, op cit., pp. 147-175.

with (a) consumption utility, (b) utility as a source of old
age security, and (c) utility as productive agents.[9] On the
other hand, children imply certain costs, both direct (i.e.,
food, clothing, education, etc.) and indirect (i.e., "...lost
opportunities as the ability of mothers to work if they must
tend to children, lost earnings during the gestation period,
or the lessened mobility of parents with large family respon-
sibilities."[10]) A model is then formulated given expectations
of the effects of increased income on the marginal utilities
and costs of a given child. Here, Leibenstein suggests that
the value of an additional child as a productive agent and
as a source of security will decline as parents' income increases, since dependence on offspring to provide these things
will have become less immediate. So far as the consumption
utility of children is concerned, Leibenstein is somewhat ob-
scure, choosing to make this factor independent of income in-
somuch as, whether higher income increases or reduces the marginal utility schedule of children, "arguments can be found
for both views".[11] On balance, then, an increase in parents'
income will lessen the importance of two of the reasons for
having children, and have an indefinite effect on the third.

Leibenstein is quite definite that a higher level of parents' income will bring about an increase in the marginal
cost schedule of children. In terms of direct costs, it is ar-
gued that parents will wish to have their children enjoy the

[9]ibid., p. 161
[10]ibid.
[11]ibid., p. 162.

same living standard as themselves. Since living standard is
expected to increase with income, therefore, we see that expenditure per child is also likely to rise. Similarly, a
greater income will broaden the range of available alternatives to children, thus increasing their indirect, or opportunity costs.

In summary, then, increases in parental income appear to
lower the marginal utility schedule, while raising the schedule of their marginal cost. It seems likely, therefore, that
an equality between the two marginal values is reached at a
smaller number of offspring than would be the case at lower
incomes.

Easterlin, an Alternative Approach to Income and the
Demand for Children: Much of the pioneering work on the economic determinants of fertility behavior has been done by
Richard Easterlin at the University of Pennsylvania. By way
of an example of Easterlin's approach, I discuss here his
analysis of the effects of per-capita income, family assets,
female labor force participation, and intended consumption
on family size in light of the post World War II 'baby boom'
(1967).[12] Easterlin begins by showing that the decline in fertility in the U.S. after 1957, despite rising real income per
capita, can be explained without having to resort to a descrip-
tion of child services as inferior goods. The following observations serve to illustrate the point:

[12] R.A. Easterlin, "On the Relation of Economic Factors to
Recent and Projected Fertility Changes",
DEMOGRAPHY, September, 1967, pp. 131-153.

(1) Most of the post-war increases in fertility, and most of the subsequent decline in the late fifties can be accounted for by those families headed by individuals between the ages of 15 and 29. Moreover, within this cohort, most of the observed changes are concentrated within the youngest sub-cohorts.[13]

(2) Using data from the Current Population Survey, Easterlin demonstrates that the fluctuations in income and wealth from the end of World War II through the early 1960's for the 15 - 29 cohort were quite consistent with the fertility behavior of that group. Specifically, incomes grew at a faster rate among this cohort than for any other age group during the late 1940's, while unemployment was lower than for any other cohort. By the late 1950's, however, income for the 14 - 29 year olds who were household heads grew more slowly than was the case for other cohorts, while unemployment came to surpass that of older families.[14]

(3) In terms of wealth, a similar picture emerged for younger families. Not only did home ownership decline for these households during the fifties (after having risen during the late forties), the proportion of these families eligible for veterans' benefits also declined.[15]

Easterlin makes what many consider to be his most interesting contribution to our understanding of fertility behavior through his consideration of the role of desired consump-

[13]ibid., pp. 132-134.

[14]ibid., pp. 135-137.

[15]ibid., p. 136.

tion. Operating on the assumption that young families strive for consumption levels achieved by their parents at the time when the former left home, Easterlin computed the ratio of Median Income for family heads aged 14 to 24, to the same for family heads aged 35 to 44. He subsequently found this ratio to have been rising during the late 1940's. From 1955 through 1962, however, it fell.[16] Consequently, during the latter period, the ability of young households to achieve their parents' consumption levels was seriously jeopardized. The simultaneous decline in fertility during that period might thus be thought of as resulting from more intense competition between numbers of children on one hand, and family status on the other.

REGRESSION ANALYSES OF FERTILITY--THE 1960'S

During the 1960's several interesting studies in which fertility behavior is made dependent on various economic and socioeconomic factors were conducted using, by and large, standard least-squares regression techniques. A common characteristic one detects in all of these is the use of intuition, rather than some theoretically rigorous model of constrained maximization, to formulate experimental hypotheses regarding coefficient signs for relevant independent variables. Since this employment of intuition appears to be Easterlin's procedure as well, I give brief note to three of these studies.[17]

---

[16]ibid., p. 137.

[17]See: Mark Perlman, "Population and Economic Change in Developing Countries: A Review Article", JOURNAL OF ECONOMIC LITERATURE (Vol. XIX, March, 1981) p. 78.

Using U.S. data (National Probability Sample--1956),
Freedman (1963)[18] offers a model whose principal asset lies in
its attempt to differentiate between the influences on fertility of family income per se, and of relative income, i.e.,
the deviation of family income from an expected value given
husband's age, education, occupation, and residence. Here,
the objective is to show that family size varies directly with,
and is sensitive to, relative rather than absolute income,
since the latter brings social pressure on the family to main-
tain status. Since status is generally demonstrated by the
possession of non-child related consumer goods, moreover, the
influence of Easterlin is quite clear.

The coefficients obtained from Freedman's regressions appear to lend some measure of support to her a priori expectations regarding the influence of relative income on fertility,
especially for families likely to have completed their fecundity (i.e., parents married over nine years).[19] In addition,
Freedman finds a weak negative correlation between a proxy for
wife's potential wage (i.e., Median Income for Working Wives
in 1955), and family size, an observation that, as is shown in
Chapter 3, anticipates the principal conclusions reached by
those who test Becker-type models.

---

[18]D.S. Freedman, "The Relation of Economic Status to Fertility",
AMERICAN ECONOMIC REVIEW, (June, 1963) pp.
414-426.

[19]Often expressed as the 'Easterlin Hypothesis', there are,
however, some who doubt its validity. See: M.R. Olneck &
B.L. Wolfe, "A Note on Some Evidence on the Easterlin Hypothesis", JOURNAL OF POLITICAL ECONOMY, (October, 1978)
pp. 953-957.

An analysis of differences in fertility behavior between
LDC's and MDC's is offered by Adelman (1963)[20]. Given U.N.
data from 37 countries, and using live births per 1000 population as the dependent variable, regression coefficients for
family income, wife's education, and urbanization are calculated. Interestingly, these coefficients are quite consistent with my own findings using different regions within the
U.S. (Chapters 5 and 6). Specifically, Adelman indicates that
family income and wife's education, while generating positive
and negative coefficients respectively, appear to have a more
significant impact on fertility behavior in LDC's that in MDC's.
As outlined in Chapter 1, and demonstrated in detail in Chapters 5 and 6, I have found the same independent variables
playing a much more profound role in family size in the Southeast, i.e., the least developed region economically, than elsewhere. Secondly, Adelman's urbanization coefficients are
negative, as expected, but stronger for MDC's than for LDC's.
Similarly, I have found urbanization to be the prime explani-
tory variable in fertility behavior in the Northeast, i.e.,
the most advanced region economically. For the Midwest and
Southeast, that variable was of marginal significance.

A final study of note is that of Friedlander & Silver
(1967).[21] Like Adelman, these authors use birth rates as the

[20] Irma Adelman, "An Econometric Analysis of Population Growth",
AMERICAN ECONOMIC REVIEW (June, 1963) pp.
314-337.

[21] S. Friedlander & M. Silver, "A Quantitative Study of the Determinants of Fertility Behavior", DEMOGRAPHY
(June, 1967) pp. 30-70.

dependent variable in regressions designed to test the interaction between economic development and the roles of factors
commonly recognized as influencing family size. Although a
formidable number and variety of independent variables are incorporated into their regressions, Friedlander & Silver find
coefficients for the majority of them to be insignificant.
Here, I shall concentrate on their findings with respect to
urbanization, parents' education, and family income.

Consistent with Adelman's results, the Friedlander &
Silver coefficients for urbanization were both negative and significant, although more so for MDC's.

Also consistent with Adelman is the relationship between
illiteracy and fertility. Recall that the latter found a significant and positive relationship for LDC's, but also one
that was rather insignificant for MDC's. Friedlander & Silver
obtain the same results. It remains to be seen, then, whether this observation is accounted for by the strong negative
relationship between illiteracy and wife's potential wage; or,
if it can be attributed to other aspects of education, i.e.,
the accessibility of contraceptive information (see: DeTray
(1973) and Michael (1973, discussed below), or perhaps, the
effect of education on the interaction of numbers with quality of Children as suggested by Becker (1981--see below).

The effect of income on fertility appears to be the most
interesting of Friedlander & Silver's findings, coefficients
for that variable being positive for LDC's and negative for

MDC's. If we assume that the earning potentials of both parents increase with development, then this observation could be interpreted as anticipating an interaction between husband's income and wife's wage of the kind predicted by Willis & Sanderson (1971), and Willis (1973--see below).

GENERAL OBSERVATIONS AND CONCLUSIONS

In this chapter I have striven to sketch a background for my own examination of fertility behavior by illustrating first the perspectives of those who have sought to define the very-long-run set of relationships running from population growth to economic development. From this point of departure, the next step was to concentrate on some of the pioneering attempts to identify those economic and socioeconomic factors significant to the determination of optimum family size at a more microeconomic level. That having been done, I proceed in Chapter 3 to discuss what to date has been the most rigorous effort to conceptualize the processes by which the family makes decisions about its size, i.e., that of Gary S. Becker.

## 3. HOUSEHOLD PRODUCTION WITH GOODS AND TIME: THE BECKER MODELS

As suggested in Chapter 2, the Easterlin-type models are quite helpful in identifying many of the socioeconomic factors instrumental in predicting fertility behavior. The inclusion of these variables was justified for the most part, however, by intuition. I proceed in this chapter, then, to discuss what I consider to be the next stage in the development of our understanding of fertility behavior. Specifically, the household is said to maximize a welfare function subject to the constraint of full family wealth. By making numbers of children and alternatives to children the arguments of this function, therefore, the effects of changes in income and other socioeconomic factors on family size can be isolated. The discussion begins with a review of Becker's own model, and then proceeds with an examination of some of the more recent theoretical and empirical variations on the Becker theme.

BECKER AND THE ALLOCATION OF TIME

In "A Theory of the Allocation of Time"[1], Becker begins by noting that economic development has greatly reduced the length of the work day. Consequently, much greater attention ought to be paid by economists to the fact that the household now has an opportunity to acquire commodities whose consumption calls for an allocation of time as well as of goods.[2] Expressing this in an orthodox format of constrained utility

[1]Gary S. Becker, "A Theory of the Allocation of Time", THE ECONOMIC JOURNAL (Sept., 1965) pp. 493-517.

[2]ibid., p. 493.

36

maximization:

$$\text{Maximize } U(Z_1, Z_2, \ldots, Z_m)$$

$$\text{Subject to: } \sum_i (p_i b_i + t_i \bar{w}) Z_i = V + T\bar{w}$$

...where the 'Z' are commodities produced in the home using inputs of goods and time, and according to the functions:

$$Z_i = f_i(x_i, T_i)$$

Here, '$f_i$' represents a production function for the creation of commodity $Z_i$, '$x_i$' is a vector of market goods required <u>per unit</u> of $Z_i$, and $T_i$ is a corresponding vector of time inputs. Becker chooses to make the latter a vector because of the heterogeneous nature of time, i.e., weekend or evening time, as opposed to weekday time.[3]

In the constraint, '$b_i$' is the vector of goods used in the total (as opposed to per unit) production of $Z_i$ such that $x_i = b_i Z_i$, while '$p_i$' is a vector of the corresponding unit prices for goods within $b_i$; '$t_i$' is a vector of time inputs required per unit of $Z_i$ such that $T_i = t_i Z_i$, and '$\bar{w}_i$' is a vector of earnings forgone per unit of $T_i$. Finally, 'V' is non-labor income, while 'T' represents a vector of total available time. $V + T\bar{w}$ can then be thought of as 'full family wealth'.

From first order maximization conditions, Becker obtains a marginal rate of substitution, $Z_i / Z_j$, which must be set equal to the ratio of 'full unit prices', where the full unit price of commodity 'i' is $p_i b_i + t_i \bar{w}$. From second order conditions, Becker can subsequently obtain changes in optimum $Z_i$

[3]ibid., p. 495.

as functions of $p_i$, $\bar{w}$, and V.[4]

A change in V results in a pure income effect which suggests a change in optimum $Z_i$ that is in the same direction as the change in V.

Given a uniform change in all elements of $\bar{w}$, a set of both substitution and income effects exists. Specifically, an increase in $\bar{w}$ has a positive income effect on the demands for all $Z_i$. The substitution effects, in contrast, are a different story. In short, if the time intensity of $Z_i$ (Fig. 3-1) is greater than that of $Z_j$, then the substitution effect is positive on the demand for the latter, but negative on that of the former.[5] Consequently, the demand for $Z_j$ rises, while the change in demand for $Z_i$ depends on which of the positive income effect or the negative substitution effect has the greater magnitude.[6]

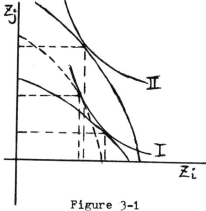

Figure 3-1

The Becker model has many applications. Labor supply, income taxation, the theory of household technology, and the computation of income elasticities are all areas for which

[4]ibid., p. 497.

[5]The illustration assumes variable factor proportions in the production functions. Thus, Samuelson-Stolper conditions should be assumed. See the discussion of the Willis model below.

[6]ibid., p. 499.

Becker demonstrates his model to have analytical value. This brings us to the principal issue at hand; that is, the applicability of Becker's model to fertility behavior.

Optimum Family Size and the Quantity-Quality Interaction:

Drawing upon earlier observations (Becker--1960), and bringing into play the concept of household production discussed above, Becker's work on fertility behavior has progressed to an analysis of the implications of an interaction between numbers of children and child quality (1973, 1981).

In his most recent model[7], Becker would have the household maximize:

$$U = U(n,q,Z)$$

...where n and q are numbers and average quality per child respectively, and 'Z' is a composite of all alternatives to child services, i.e., 'Living Standard'.[8]

Maximization is then said to be constrained by the function:

$$p_n n + p_q q + p_c(q)qn + pZ = I$$

...where 'I' is full family wealth as defined previously, and 'p' is the shadow price of alternatives to children. Here, Becker defines '$p_n$' as an average fixed cost per child reflecting "...the time, expenditure, discomfort, and risk spent in pregnancy and delivery, governmental child allowances..., the costs of avoiding pregnancies and deliveries, and all other

[7]Gary S. Becker, A TREATISE ON THE FAMILY, Cambridge, Mass., Harvard University Press, 1981.

[8]ibid., p. 95.

psychic and monetary expenditures on children that are largely independent of quality."[9] '$p_q$' represents expenditures on quality that are independent of numbers of children, i.e., hand-me-down clothes, learning from parents, etc. Finally, Becker suggests a divergence of marginal from average variable costs of quality because of such factors as public subsidies to schooling, etc. This is represented by the function '$p_c(q)$'.

Upon calculation of first-order maximization conditions, Becker shows that the ratio of shadow prices of numbers to quality depends on the ratio of quality to numbers as expected, but also varies directly with the ratio of fixed to variable cost of quantity, and inversely with the ratios of (a) fixed to variable cost of quality, and (b) marginal variable cost to average variable cost of quality.[10] Some interesting implications stem from this observation.

First, the quantity-quality interaction serves to intensify the substitution effect away from numbers given an increase in $p_n$, even when the elasticity of substitution between quantity and quality is small. Thus, an increase in the market value of wife's time (assuming that child rearing is indeed time intensive) could generate a substitution effect that is much stronger than would be the case without the quantity-quality interaction, and is thus more likely to offset the income effect so far as numbers of children is concerned.

---

[9]ibid., p. 108.

[10]ibid., p. 107.

Secondly, it is possible that a 'pure' rise in income could raise the rate of return on child quality. Consequently, a decline in the demand for numbers of children may occur, even though the 'true' income elasticity of demand for children is positive and large.[11]

In addition to its impact on the relationship between such factors as wife's wage and husband's income, and family size, Becker's quantity-quality interaction has implications for the roles of variables such as urbanization, child mortality, and parents' education.

With respect to urbanization, Becker suggests two reasons why rural families within developed economies tend to be larger than their urban counterparts. First, there is the obvious excess in material productivity of rural as opposed to urban children. Thus, the net fixed cost of the former is less than that of the latter. Secondly, economic development in Becker's words "raises the rates of return on education and other training of <u>urban</u> children..."[12] Since this implies a reduction in the marginal cost of quality, the substitution effect arising from the quantity-quality interaction presents itself once more.

Becker is skeptical of conclusions drawn from empirical evidence that a direct path of causation exists from parents' to children's education.[13] Rather, the interaction suggests that the negative relationship between parents' education and

---

[11]ibid., p. 112.

[12]ibid., p. 110.

[13]ibid., p. 113.

quantity of children (see the discussion of Michael's observations, below) creates a substitution effect in favor of
children's education, i.e., child quality.

Finally, Becker's interaction has implications surrounding the relationship between child mortality and family size.
If, for example, measures designed to reduce child mortality
are used by parents, then $p_n$ rises since each child is now
more likely to reach maturity.[14] Thus, by treating children's
life expectancy as an aspect of child quality, we see once
again that Becker's analysis is applicable.

SUBSEQUENT VARIATIONS OF THE BECKER MODEL

Having discussed Becker's foundations for a theoretically
rigorous examination of fertility behavior, I now consider some
variations of the Becker theme. Included here are brief out-
lines of T.P. Schultz' observations on the role of infant mortality, Willis' differentiation of the behavior of working as
opposed to non-working wives, DeTray's concentration on child
quality, and Michael's investigation of the effect of education
on the costs of contraceptive information.

T.P. Schultz and Child Mortality: An early attempt to in-
vestigate fertility behavior from the perspective of family
welfare maximization is offered by T.P. Schultz.[15] Specifically, the family tries to maximize a utility function whose
arguments are children, and presumably, some substitute for

---

[14]ibid., p. 112.

[15]T.P. Schultz, "An Economic Model of Family Planning and Fertility", JOURNAL OF POLITICAL ECONOMY (April,
1969) pp. 153-180.

child services, subject to the family's full wealth. The cost
of raising children is then expressed as a function of several
independent variables including wife's potential income, the
material productivity of children, other sources of family income, educational achievement of parents, desired education
for children, and institutions surrounding the array of social
services.[16]

As suggested by Becker's work, and reiterated by those
whose efforts are discussed below, increases in wife's wage potential will, by raising the opportunity cost of children, tend
to reduce the demand for numbers of them. In contrast, the
availability of income opportunities for children should, by
lowering their net cost, make them more attractive sources of
utility.

Schultz also gives recognition to the interrelationship between income, status, and desired consumption. While changes
in permanent income would, ceteris paribus, tend to cause an
adjustment in desired family size in the same direction, such
changes would also induce a reevaluation of social expectations, thus making the ceteris paribus assumption unwarranted.
This, of course, is a restatement of Easterlin's hypothesis.

The achievement by parents of greater levels of education
tends, in Schultz' opinion, to reduce optimum family size
through the greater exposure of educated parents to contraceptive technology. Schultz goes on to suggest that higher levels
of education for children (even when provided by the state) tend

---

[16]ibid., p. 154.

to lower optimum fertility as well; his argument being that
children's education will (a) reduce their current income earning abilities, and (b) create the necessity for expenditures
on clothing, school supplies, etc. Apparently, Schultz assumes that the discounted future earning power of educated (as
opposed to uneducated) children is of negligible importance in
the family planning decision.

Social institutions can play a significant role in the
formulation of an optimum fertility plan. As retirement insurance becomes more readily available, for example, the value
of large numbers of children as a form of 'social security' becomes less significant (see Leibenstein, above). The existence
(and enforcement) of child labor laws could have a similar effect on fertility as such legislation renders children less
valuable as sources of current income. On the other hand, it
is conceivable that programs which provide aid to families with
dependent children may, by lowering the net cost of them to parents, stimulate fertility. This of course was Malthus' argument in opposition to the Poor Laws.

Finally, Schultz' most interesting contribution, I believe,
is his analysis of the role of child mortality. Specifically,
a change in the rate of child deaths can have distinctive effects on long-run family planning. Here, sociological arrangements such as age of first marriage are the principal areas of
influence. For example, an increase in infant life expectancy
could enable young adults to postpone marriage, and still

44

achieve a target family size. In the context of Becker's model of time allocation, a decline in that dimension of the time vector (T) which one might refer to as 'fecundity time' would have a negative income effect on the total demand for numbers of children over the lifetime of the household, with reduced child mortality insuring that the number of children who survive to adulthood is maintained. Thus, a question of uncertainty is raised. Since a higher infant death rate tends to increase the variance on a given expected level of fertility, it seems likely that various social factors influence fertility by instilling within family planners attitudes about how to compensate for this risk. Consequently, a willingness to tolerate a larged anticipated family in order to insure against a less than optimum number of children, for example, would imply a relatively strong correlation between infant mortality and fertility.

The Rybczynski Effect in Household Production: Willis & Sanderson (1971)[17] and Willis (1973)[18] have presented Becker-type models offering rigorous differentiations between (a) the demands for numbers of children (N) and child quality (Q), and (b) the income elasticity of demand for 'Child Services' (i.e., the product N x Q) for working as opposed to nonworking wives. While a mere sketch of the latter modification is provided by Willis & Sanderson, a more complete discussion of both

[17]R.J. Willis & W. Sanderson, "Economic Models of Fertility: Some Examples and Implications", NATIONAL BUREAU OF ECONOMIC RESEARCH (51st Annual Report, Sept., 1971) pp. 32-42.

[18]R.J. Willis, op cit.

points is given by Willis. It is on this latter work, therefore, that I concentrate attention here.

Willis begins with the problem of maximizing a household
welfare function subject to the Becker-type constraints in
which arguments are manufactured at home using as inputs limited supplies of market goods and time. Stated formally:

$$\text{Maximize: } U = U(C,s)$$
$$\text{where} \quad C = N \times Q$$
$$\text{Subject to: } F(NQ,S,H,k,T) = 0$$

...where the constraint, F, is a standard production possibilities function.[19] Here, 'H' represents the sum of husband's
lifetime earnings plus outside sources of wealth, 'k' is a
shift parameter determining wife's wage potential, and 'T' is
wife's lifetime allocation of time.

Next, demand functions for child services and living standard are written:

$$C = C(I,p_c,p_s)$$
$$= N(I,p_c,p_s)Q(I,p_c,p_s)$$
$$S = S(I,p_c,p_s)$$

...where $p_c$ and $p_s$ are shadow prices of child services and
living standard, and 'I' is full family wealth.

Pointing out that optimum demands occur at the point of
equality between rates of commodity substitution and rates of
product transformation, Willis proceeds to consider the effects
of changes in family wealth and shadow prices on the demand for
child services in general, and for numbers of children in particular.

[19]ibid., p. 24.

Using the specification, $C = N \times Q$, it may be concluded
that the wealth elasticity of C is equal to the sum of the
wealth elasticities of N and Q. Thus, if Becker's empirical
conclusion that Q is more wealth elastic than N[20] is valid, a
plausible argument can be made that the wealth elasticity of N
could even be negative, implying that children in terms of numbers are an inferior good, although child services is not.

To obtain the effects of a change in the shadow price of
child services, Willis refers to Theil (1952) to suggest that
second-order maximization conditions dictate (a) that the compensated substitution effect on either of N or Q may be positive, but not on both, and (b) whether either is indeed positive will depend on their relationship as substitutes or complements. Specifically, if N and Q are complements, then both
compensated substitution effects are negative. Pointing to
arguments by Deusenbury (1960) and Blake (1968) that Q is more
likely to reflect parents' living standard, and thus move with
S, it follows then that substitution effects are positive for
Q and negative for N.

Considered next is the effect of a change in wife's wage
on desired fertility. To begin, the influence of a change in
wife's wage (W) on $p_c$ must be determined. While this would be
a fairly simple matter were factor proportions in household
production to be fixed, the issue is slightly more complicated
should variable proportions be the rule. Fortunately, Samuelson & Stolper (1941) show that if (a) all production func-

---

[20]Becker, op cit (1960).

tions are linear homogeneous, (b) factor intensities differ, and (c) factor intensity ordering is invariant over the entire range of factor price ratios, then there will exist a monotonic relationship between the value of wife's time, her wage, and the shadow price of child services, again assuming the production of the latter to be time intensive relative to living standard. Consequently, an increase in W generates positive income effects on N and Q, and a substitution effect that is negative for N, and whose magnitude varies directly with the degree to which parents consider quality to be a substitute for quantity.

I believe Willis makes his most significant contribution by illustrating how the form of the constraint in the maximization problem can be made dependent upon wife's labor force participation.[21] If, for example, the wife does in fact choose to be employed, especially for an extended part of her married life, then the wage she can expect to earn becomes endogenous, work experience making a positive contribution to the shift parameter, k, defined above. Here, the constraint may be re-arranged and expressed as:

$$0 = F(NQ,S,H,k,T) = J(S,H,k,T) - C$$

...where the wife equates the marginal value of a unit of time (W) to the market wage (W').[22] Hereafter, this is referred to

---

[21] It might be of interest to speculate on those factors that could affect that wage at which the wife would decide to enter the labor force. See Gronau (1973).

[22] Willis, op cit, p. 36.

as Willis' 'J' constraint. If, on the other hand, the wife
finds it preferable not to work, she reveals that W exceeds
W', even though all of her time is spent in home production.
Here:

$$0 = F(NQ,S,H,k,T) = K(S,H,T) - C$$

i.e., Willis' 'K' constraint.[23] It is with this latter case
that an interesting phenomenon occurs. Specifically:

> "An increase in the husband's lifetime income, H,
> increases the family's supply of goods...but leaves
> the supply of wife's time unaffected..., while in
> T, the wife's life-span after marriage, increases
> the supply of time without affecting the supply of
> goods. An important property of the K-type con-
> straint is that an increase in the supply of goods
> (time) will tend to raise (lower) the opportunity
> cost of children unless the output of C (S) falls
> absolutely by a sufficient amount. This property,
> often called Rybczynski's theorem, follows from
> the assumption that $p_c$ exceeds $p_s$..."[24]

The significance of this statement is clear. That is, if husband's income rises, given the wife's absence from the labor
market, then we may observe a decline in fertility, not because children are an inferior good, but rather because of
substitution effects favoring the demands for goods-intensive
commodities.

As stated previously, this final point was first articu-
lated by Willis & Sanderson (1971). Both the earlier and this
more recent of theoretical presentations were followed, moreover, by the design and testing of an econometric model constructed with this interaction between husband's income and
wife's wage in mind. Both are discussed later in this chapter.

---

[23]ibid.

[24]ibid., p. 44.

DeTray, Non-Income Factors: An Active Husband Model:

DeTray (1973) offers a model differing from Willis' in three respects.[25] First, he chooses to use an 'active husband' in child services production. That is, husband's time is included along with wife's time and goods in the production functions for numbers of children (N) and child quality (Q). Secondly, child services is expressed at the more general C = C(N,Q), rather than Willis' more specific C = N x Q. Finally, household production is constrained by full wealth, expressed by DeTray as the sum of the values of mother's and father's available time ($W_m$ and $W_f$), plus non-labor income (V). This in turn is equal to the sum of the products of commodity demands and commodity shadow prices, i.e., $p_c C + p_z Z$.[26]

Upon determining welfare maximization conditions, DeTray proceeds to make a number of observations. First, in the case of demand for numbers of children, unambiguous signs are obtained only for the effects of changes in the price of child related goods (negative), and non-labor income (positive), the offsetting substitution and income effects of a change in $W_m$ being a common characteristic of these types of models. Of course, the same sort of offsetting influences occur given a change in $W_f$, this being an 'active husband' model. A second, and perhaps more unique outcome of the solution to DeTray's constrained maximization problem is that parents' education, via an influence on production efficiency can affect family size

[25]D. DeTray, "Child Quality and the Demand for Children", JOURNAL OF POLITICAL ECONOMY (Supplement, March/April, 1973) pp. 70-95.

[26]ibid., p. 72

in a way that is independent of the more obvious connection between schooling and income earning ability. Recall this point being made during the discussion of Schultz' work. Here, DeTray suggests several possibilities. Pointing to studies by Cohen, Rea, and Lerman (1970), and by Leibowitz (1972) suggesting that highly educated women tend to devote more time to the rearing of an additional child than do less educated women, and postulating himself that the time efficiency in child quality production improves with wife's education, the conclusion is reached that wife's education is not factor neutral in its effect on the efficiency of household production.

DeTray completes his theoretical considerations of fertility behavior by making a brief examination of the effects of urbanization and infant mortality. With respect to the former, three possible reasons within the context of the model are given to account for the larger family sizes observed to occur in rural areas. First, there is the traditional argument that children are more valuable as sources of family income on the farm than they are in the city. DeTray is skeptical of this explanation, however, noting:

> "One implication of the traditional argument, therefore, is that the elasticity of substitution between child time and 'hired' time is larger than that between child-time and adult home-time. If this were not true, parents who live in urban areas could substitute the child-time for their own time in the home, enabling them to allocate more hours to work. Thus, in household production models rural child-time plays conceptually much the same role as urban child-time in the household decision-making process, reducing the expected difference from this source."[27]

[27]ibid., pp. 77-78.

A second possibility for the urban-rural difference is that the shadow price of children could be lower on the farm, especially if opportunities exist for the mother to participate simultaneously in home and family business activities. Finally, DeTray points to the likelihood that in rural areas the cost of child quality is higher relative to numbers of children than in urban areas, basic food, shelter, etc. being less expensive on the farm, while quality items such as education, travel, etc. are more expensive there.

With respect to child mortality, DeTray appears willing to accept conventional expectations that parents compensate for infant deaths by having more children (see Schultz, above). He qualifies this acceptance, however, by suggesting that we must assume that (a) the cost of infant death must be zero, and (b) the mortality elasticity of demand for surviving children must also be zero. In other words, expenditures for children who fail to survive must not reduce family income so much that 'replacements' cannot be afforded; and parents must not wish to insure against more (fewer) than the optimum number of surviving children by planning too few (too many) births (see the discussion of maximization under conditions of uncertainty--Chapter 4).

Michael, Education and Contraception: As stated earlier, Michael gives us a model in which parents' education affects fertility through its relationship with the availability of contraceptive information.[28] Like the other models discussed here,

---

[28]R. Michael, "Education and the Derived Demand for Children", JOURNAL OF POLITICAL ECONOMY (Supplement, March/April, 1973) pp. 128-164.

a statement is made defining a problem of constrained welfare maximization in the context of household production. In Michael's version, however, welfare function arguments are distributed over the household's lifetime, and as such, present values are used to express flows associated with price, wage, and property income variables within the constraint. Attention is then focused on two of the utility function arguments, i.e., 'family life' and 'sexual gratification'. These are represented by $Z_1$ and $Z_2$ respectively.

The treatment of child services is fairly standard, $Z_1$ being made a function of goods, time, and child services (C). 'C' is then expressed as the product of a proportionality factor, 'a', and number of children (N), and is produced according to a function containing goods, time, and an element representing family environment (e).

After stating that sexual gratification ($Z_2$) is also produced in the home using inputs of goods and time, Michael proceeds to write a function expressing the probability of conception per unit time as dependent on inputs of goods and time ($x_p$ and $T_p$), as well as sexual gratification and parents' unadjusted fecundity (F), i.e.,

$$P = f(x_p, T_p; Z_2, F)$$

...where P is expected to vary directly with $Z_2$ and F.[29]

Next, a function for direct expenditure on conception probability given $Z_2$ and F is set down:

---

[29] ibid., p. 131.

$$G/_{Z_2, F} = \Pi_p(P-P^*) = x_p p_x + T_p$$

...where $\Pi_p$ is the price of a unit change in P, P* is the level
of P that would have existed given F and $Z_2$ had G been zero,
and $p_x$ and $T_p$ are input prices.[30] Since G must be non-negative,
it is specified that the sign of $\Pi_p$ is the same as that of
(P-P*).

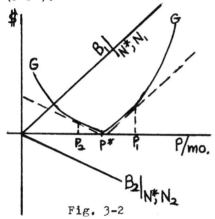

Fig. 3-2

Given the cost of fertility control, optimum expenditure for
the latter can be determined as
illustrated in Figure 3-2.[31] Here,
the cost function, G, appears
with two alternative benefit
functions, $B_1$ and $B_2$, each of
which is derived from the household's excess demand for children
during the current decision period. $B_1$, for example, implies
that the desired number of children, $N_1$, exceeds the current
number of offspring, N*, its positive slope indicating the de-
sirability of an increased probability of conception. Alternatively, $B_2$ suggests that optimum number of children, $N_2$, is
less than N*. Michael does not explain the linear relationship
between B and P, so we must assume this to have been done for
simplicity. Having plotted benefit and cost functions of P,
therefore, it is a simple matter to equate marginal values to

[30] ibid.

[31] ibid., p. 133.

find optimum conception probabilities, i.e., $P_1$ and $P_2$. Here, we see that parents with a positive excess demand for children would seek to improve the probability of conception to a point beyond P*, i.e., to $P_1$. $P_2$ would then be the target probability for parents who feel that their family size is excessive.

Michael's next step is to consider the role of education in fertility planning. Here, a wide range of possibilities are discussed, including the effects of education on the utility function, the wealth constraint, and the production function constraints. For the latter, special attention is given to child quality and fertility control.

With respect to the utility function, Michael finds it necessary to avoid a priori predictions since such would require a viable theory about the formation of preferences, a theory which does not currently exist.[32]

Within the wealth constraint, the human capital arising from education is unique since its effect on the opportunity cost of time differs from that of other assets. Specifically, Michael argues, the income flow from human capital, unlike other types of assets, cannot be seperated from the use of one's time. Furthermore, if the productivity of human capital is not homogeneous among the various uses of time, and if it depreciates from non-use in those areas for which it is especially adapted, i.e., time spent on child rearing rather than on various labor market activities, then we conclude that child rearing demands a high user cost of this type of human capital.

[32]ibid., p. 134.

This is essentially the conclusion speculated on by DeTray. That is, the effects of education on household production tend to favor child quality and living standard rather than numbers of children.

The latter argument is important because its implication that educated parents prefer fewer children leads us directly to the question of education and fertility control. Here, the significance is clear. Specifically, Michael cites several studies showing that familiarity with, and willingness to use contraceptive techniques vary directly with educational achievement.[33] Since this suggests a reduction in the cost of fertility control, therefore, it follows that, for better educated parents, optimum P varies considerably more from P* than for less educated families. Graphically, this is shown by having the cost function, G, drawn less steeply to both the left and the right of P*. Now, considering the previous arguments suggesting that educated parents prefer fewer children, we see that for a given benefit function, say $B_2$ in Figure 3-2, optimum P ($=P_2$) would be farther to the left of P* than for less educated parents. Thus, the probability of unwanted children being conceived during the decision period is reduced.

In summary, then, Michael's model suggests (a) that better educated parents are more likely to attempt to avoid conception during a given time period, and (b) they are more likely to achieve this objective.

---

[33]ibid., p. 141.

Here, then, the effects of education, a sketch for which is provided by DeTray, are seen to be treated with a still greater degree of rigor. In my own model (Chapter 4), I make liberal use of the theoretical treatment of education established here.

ECONOMETRIC TESTS OF THE BECKER MODELS

Having reviewed the theoretical side of the Becker-type models, I now consider some efforts to examine econometrically the hypotheses of those models.

Schultz and Family Size in Puerto Rico: According to Schultz, it will be recalled, fertility behavior is affected by several independent variables, i.e., those surrounding the mean and variance of infant mortality, as well as those affecting the cost of raising children. Given a Becker-type problem of constrained welfare maximization, the solution to which is expected to depend on the latter sets of factors, Schultz proceeds to specify and test an econometric representation of his model.[34]

Schultz' findings, using data drawn from 75 Puerto Rican municipalities (1951 through 1957) provide strong evidence of the role of death rates in fertility planning, at least in a developing country. Thus, support is given to a priori expectations that higher fertility rates in LDC's are in part intended to compensate for higher rates of infant mortality. On the other hand, Schultz' regressions show no strong correlation

---

[34]Schultz, op cit.

between 'uncertainty', as represented by the variance on infant death rates, and planned family size. Apparently, no strong tendency exists among those comprising Schultz' sample to insure against non-optimum family size by adjusting the number of births.

Schultz calculates significant and negative coefficients between family size and both parents' and children's education, relationships interpreted by Becker (see above) as indicating the role of education in the quantity-quality interaction.

While the coefficient of family income is significant at 5%, its negative sign leads Schultz, quite rightly, to suspect interference with the adult education term.[35] Indeed, the absolute value of the latter factor's coefficient is sharply reduced with the inclusion of the income variable. This is a frequent consequence of multicollinearity.

Finally, Schultz' coefficients for the proportion of married women who are working are negative as might be expected given the assumption that child rearing is time intensive. Unfortunately, significant coefficients were not obtained for urbanization, agricultural background, or for the proportion of the adult population that is married.

Willis, Willis & Sanderson: Interaction Among Income Variables: The principal feature of Willis' model was its suggestion that husband's income could exert a negative influence

[35]ibid., p. 170

on fertility through a Rybczynski effect should the wife choose
not to participate in the labor force. This same theme was
initially developed in an earlier paper by Willis & Sanderson.[36]

Using data from the one-in-one-thousand sample of the 1960
Census of Population, and from a five percent sample compiled
by the Ruggles' for North Central States in 1940, Willis &
Sanderson construct and test an econometric model in which number of children (N) is made a linear function of wife's wage (W)
and husband's earning power (H). Wife's years of education was
used as a proxy for W, while 'last year's income' represented
H. The following specification was made:

$$N = a + bH + cW + d(HxW) \quad (37)$$

The interaction term, HxW, reflects the effect discussed above
in which W influences the responsiveness of N to changes in H,
i.e., $\partial N/\partial H = b + dW$. The model was tested with and without
this interaction term.

The results obtained were quite consistent with those expected. In the non-interaction model, the sign of 'c' was negative and significant for all age cohorts for both 1960 and 1940
data. The coefficient of H was negative and significant for
the three oldest cohorts for 1940, and for the oldest 1960 cohort. For younger age groups, however, significance is absent.

---

[36]ibid., p. 35. Note: In Willis' later paper, a quadratic form
is considered ideal. The shorter specification is used,
however, because of 'unavoidable imprecision in the definition of the variables'. (Willis, op cit, pp. 46-47).

[37]Willis & Sanderson, op cit.

In contrast, 'b' and 'c' were negative and significant for all cohorts (both censuses) in the interaction model. As expected, the coefficient for the interaction term, 'd', was positive and significant for all cohorts for both 1940 and 1960. Thus, as expected, the change in fertility resulting from a change in husband's income varies directly with wife's wage. For sufficiently low values of W, however, it appears that the negative substitution effect on fertility resulting from increases in H outweighs the positive income effect.

In his later paper, Willis uses the same interaction specification as with Sanderson earlier, although an additional variable, SMSA, with values 1,2,3, or 4 was used to 'hold the influence of the size of urban area' constant.[38] Again, coefficients for both H and W are found to be negative and significant, while the coefficient of HxW is positive and significant. Also significant is the SMSA coefficient (negative). Of special interest, however, is that the coefficient of H is substantially more significant when 'expected income at age 40' is used as a proxy, rather than 'reported income in 1959', indicating, as might be expected, that fertility behavior is more clearly related to a 'lifetime concept of income' rather than to current income.[39] Finally, Willis points out that the effect of husband's income becomes positive at a wife's education level of about twelve years. Thus, for less educated populations, it is suggested that income growth reduces fertility, while higher degrees of formal education appear to be

---

[38]Willis, op cit, p. 51     [39]ibid., p. 52

conducive to a positive income effect.

DeTray, Number of Children and Child Quality: In his
theoretical model, DeTray speculates on the several influences of parents' education, urbanization, infant mortality, and
of course, parents' earning ability on both numbers of children
and child quality. His econometric model is designed to test
the effects of these independent variables on each of the latter welfare function arguments. To represent dependent variables, DeTray uses children-ever-born per 1000 women aged 35 -
44 (1960) for numbers of children, and the product of expected
years of public schooling per child and expected county expenditure on education per child per year for child quality.[40]
Recognizing that a bias may be possible given the endogenous
nature of earnings, DeTray uses both Ordinary and Second Stage
Least Squares estimates of coefficients. His findings indicate:

(1) Male education has no significant effect on fertility
(both OLS & 2SLS), and only a marginally significant negative
effect ($t=-1.77$) on child quality in the OLS estimate.

(2) Female education is significantly correlated in both
estimates with both dependent variables. As expected, the correlation is negative for numbers of children, and positive for
child quality.

(3) Housing value (a proxy for family wealth) is positively correlated with fertility, and significant in both estimates,
but does not appear to play a major role in the demand for child
quality.

[40] DeTray, op cit, p. 80.

(4) Male earnings have a significant and positive effect on fertility. The correlation with quality is also positive, but significant in the OLS estimate only.

(5) Female earnings have a strong negative effect on number of children (t=-12.5 for OLS and -13.2 for 2SLS). There is, however, no significant effect on child quality.

(6) The infant death rate has no effect on fertility, and a negative and significant effect on child quality.

(7) As anticipated, urbanization has a negative influence on fertility; but unexpectedly, it has no significant effect on child quality.

(8) Finally, proxies designed to represent farm background and racial composition proved to have little significance on the demands for either numbers or quality of children.

In general, DeTray's findings are consistent with expectations stated earlier. More importantly, they suggest that fertility is influenced more by female rather than by male related variables. With respect to child quality, on the other hand, the results are less clear. The reason for this, DeTray admits, quite possibly lies with the proxy used, i.e., public school expenditures. Perhaps if data were available for total educational expenditure (i.e., both public and private, as well as higher education), this proxy might have yielded better results.

Gardner: The Behavior of Rural Families: Since the three regions included in my own study (Chapters 5 and 6) reflect

varying degrees of rural influence, it might be useful to examine Gardner's analysis of a population that is primarily
rural.[41]

Gardner begins by providing a brief summary of the standard
model of household production, suggesting that his objective is
not to add materially to the theoretical contributions of others, but rather to apply the model itself to rural data. Recognizing the endogenous nature of several of the variables
tested, and hesitating to accept the assumption that child
rearing is time intensive, Gardner refuses to state any a priori predictions about coefficient signs.

Data are selected from interviews of individual rural (farm
and non-farm) families in North Carolina, and sixteen seperate regressions are run using alternative specifications of
variables in various combinations. Several independent factors are, however, common to all of the regressions. These are:
husband's and wife's schooling, wife's age, race, and family
income. In addition, three wage variables are also considered.
These are:

(1) Wife's Wage: This is used in regressions confined to
families for which the wife had participated to some degree in
the labor market during the previous year.

(2) County Wage: This is included as an alternative to
wife's wage, and is a representation of the prevailing wage in
the local labor market.

---

[41] Bruce Gardner, "Economics of the Size of North Carolina Rural
Families", JOURNAL OF POLITICAL ECONOMY,
(Supplement, March/April, 1973) pp. 99-122.

(3) Husband's Wage: Less attention is paid to this variable than to wife's wage. It is used quite probably to cover the possibility that husband's time is an input in the rearing of children.

Along with the several variable combinations used, a number of subsamples are tested individually, i.e., non-white families, farm families, and families with at least one child.

To summarize Gardner's results, consider first the five common independent variables.

(1) Wife's schooling has a negative effect on fertility in all but one of the sixteen regressions, although lower levels of significance occured in those regressions for which wife's wage was included. This is to have been expected given the positive correlation between wife's schooling and her wage.

(2) Husband's schooling is also negatively correlated with number of children (all regressions). Consistent with DeTray's findings, 't' values here are generally lower than for coefficients of wife's schooling. Of some interest here, however, is the fact that this variable is of much greater significance for farm families than is wife's education. Here, an important behavioral difference between farm and non-farm families may have been observed.

(3) Wife's age, a proxy for completed fertility, behaves as expected, yielding positive coefficients in all regressions.

(4) The non-white attribute in Gardner's regressions produced, in contrast to those of DeTray, strongly positive co-

efficients for all regressions in which non-white families were not examined exclusively.

(5) Family income produced significant and positive co-efficients in all regressions for which it was included.

With respect to the three wage variables:

(1) Wife's wage is negatively correlated with number of children in all of the four regressions where it appeared, although 't' values were substantially lower than those determined by Willis, Willis & Sanderson, and DeTray.

(2) County wage was used to compensate for spurious correlations between wife's wage and non-economic variables, and fertility. In each of the nine regressions in which it was included, a negative coefficient occured, but was of a level of significance only marginally greater than were coefficients of wife's wage.

(3) Husband's wage was included in eight regressions. While its coefficient was negative in all cases, it was significant in just two of them. Like the schooling variables, then, this is consistent with DeTray's conclusion that female related variables tend to play a more important role in family planning than do their male counterparts.

Farm families seem from Gardner's regressions to behave in a manner that is different from that of the general population in two respects. First, they appear to constitute an exception to the rule that female education is of greater importance to fertility behavior than is male education; and secondly, farm families seem to complete their fertility earlier than do others.

While the behavior of non-whites does not digress from that of the general population so far as male-female education effects are concerned, this group does appear to share with farm families the tendency to complete their fertility more quickly.

Cain & Dooley, Fleisher & Rhodes: Simultaneous Estimation: Since the early 1970's, research into Becker-type models of fertility behavior has taken two alternative though similar directions. One line of inquiry, for example, involves the allocation of wife's time to child rearing and labor force activity over the life cycle of the family. Here, the works of McCurdy (1981), Heckman (1976), Ward & Butz (1980), and Rosenzweig & Wolpin (1980) come to mind as being especially valuable. The second direction taken involves the simultaneous estimation of such factors as numbers of children, child quality, wife's wage, and wife's labor supply. Specific examples here include work done by Fleisher & Rhodes (1979), and by Cain & Dooley (1976). Since this path of investigation is more consistent with the long-run time context in which I am interested, a word or two on these latter efforts is offered here.

Cain & Dooley[42]: The objective of these authors is to generate a multi-staged least-square method for the simultaneous estimation of fertility, wife's wage, and wife's labor

[42]Glen Cain & Martin Dooley, "Estimation of a Model of Labor Supply, Fertility, and Wages of Married Women", JOURNAL OF POLITICAL ECONOMY (Sept., 1976) pp. 179-199.

66

supply. As such, the following variables are identified:

L=Labor Force Participation of Married Women
C=Percent of Children in Parochial School (i.e., a proxy for
Catholicism)
D=Disabilities among Married Women
F=Fertility            N=Other Family Income
W=Wife's Wage          R=Rural Residence
H=Husband's Income     I=Industry Mix (i.e., Demand)
E=Wife's Education     U=Male Unemployment Rate

...and the following functions are specified:

$$L = L(F,W,H,N,E,U,D)$$
$$F = F(W,L,H,N,E,C,R)$$
$$W = W(F,L,E,U,I)$$

In general, the signs of coefficients of independent variables
common to the fertility equation in this model and my own an-
ticipations regarding the demand for progeny are expected to
be the same, i.e., the impacts on F of H, N, and R should be
positive, while those of E and L are anticipated to be negative. The variable, C, is used here as a proxy for the extent
of Catholicism, which in turn, is meant to represent religious
traditionalism. The coefficient of C is expected to be positive. Finally, the authors assume child rearing to be time intensive, and that the substitution effect of a change in W has
a greater magnitude than the income effect. Thus, a negative
correlation is predicted to exist between W and F.

To test each of the three equations in their model, Cain
& Dooley draw upon the 1970 Census of Population (SMSA's over
250,000 population).

By way of results, significant coefficients were obtained
for wife's wage, husband's income, male unemployment, and female disability in the labor force regression. With the excep-

tion of the coefficient of female disability, all of the latter had expected signs. The authors believe, moreover, that the disability coefficient anomaly is the result of work disabilities being highly correlated with age, which in turn, is positively correlated, at least to a point, with labor force participation.

Within the fertility regression, coefficients of W, N, and E were significant. As expected, the W coefficient was negative so that consistency with the effect of wife's wage in the labor supply regression is maintained. While the effect of other family income (N) on fertility proved to be positive, as expected, regressions here produce education coefficients that are also positive. No explanation is offered by the authors for this peculiarity. Finally, a weak coefficient for husband's income in fertility regressions leads to the suspicion that some input of husband's time is widely recognized as necessary to child rearing. This is consistent with observations made by DeTray and Gardner (both theoretical and empirical, see above).

The final set of regressions run by Cain & Dooley are intended to test the equation for wife's wage. Here, coefficients were significant and of expected signs for L, F, and E. In all other cases, insignificant coefficients were obtained.

Fleisher & Rhodes:[43] As with Cain & Dooley, the objective

[43]Belton Fleisher & George Rhodes, "Fertility, Women's Wage Rates, and Labor Supply", AMERICAN ECONOMIC REVIEW (March, 1979) pp. 14-24.

of these authors is to estimate a series of simultaneous relationships among which are fertility, wife's wage, and wife's labor force participation. The Fleisher & Rhodes model goes a step further, however, in its incorporation of an equation representing child quality demand.

The discussion begins with the expression of an explicitly Becker-type problem of utility maximization in which Child Services, Child Quality, and Alternatives to Children are sources of satisfaction, and are produced with inputs of goods and wife's time. It is assumed that the production of child services is relatively time intensive.

Next, four endogenous and five exogenous variables are identified. The former include Wife's Wage (WM), Number of Children Ever Born (N), Child Quality (Q) as represented by the wage rates of young adults, and Wife's Labor Market Experience (R) as measured by the percent of years worked since leaving school. Exogenous variables include Husband's Wage at Age 40 (WF), Wife's Age (A), Wife's Education (SM), Husband's Education (SF), and a dummy factor (=1) for Blacks (B). Four linear equations are then expressed such that:

$$\ln WM = WM(WF, SM, B, R, NR)$$
$$N = N(WMQ, WF, A, SF, B)$$
$$Q = Q(WMN, WF, SM, B)$$
$$R = R(WN, N, Q, WF, A, SM, B)$$

Here, the first and fourth equations represent the outcome of wife's investment in human capital and her labor market experience respectively. While the expectations of coefficient signs are fairly routine, the interaction term, NR, in the wage equation does require some explanation. Following the lead of Mincer & Polachek (1974), Fleisher & Rhodes suggest that, while wife's work experience since leaving school is expected to contribute positively to her earning power, a large family tends to detract from her ability to acquire the same degree of on-the-job training as would have been the case were she to have had fewer children.

The second equation is designed to explain fertility behavior. Here, the product, WMQ, is used to represent the cost of raising children of a desired quality. Since the latter is multiplied by the market value of wife's time, moreover, it is clearly implied that, contrary to my own child premium (see Chapter 4), child quality is assumed to be time intensive. The coefficient of WMQ is thus expected to be negative. Coefficients of WF and A are expected to be positive for obvious reasons, while that of SF is hypothesized to be negative. In the latter case, the rationale lies with exposure to contraceptive information. The coefficient of B can be of either sign, its value reflecting cultural differences that may affect fertility.

Child Quality is described in the third equation. Again, coefficients of husband's wage and mother's education are expected to be positive, and again, the effect of race is uncertain given the exogenous nature of cultural differences. The coefficient of the product, WMN, is also expected to assume either sign. This is because total child quality, while expected to rise with the number of children, is postulated to be time intensive. Thus, a higher wage tends to reduce incentives to invest time in the improvement of children.

Fleisher & Rhodes use data from National Longitudinal Surveys, in contrast to the aggregative data employed by Cain & Dooley, as well as by myself.

By far, the most successful of the four tests was that for the human capital equation. Here, all coefficient signs were significant and consistent with prior expectations. The B coefficient was negative, and the most significant factor was the product, NR. The least important factor, on the other hand, was husband's wage which, while at the margin of statistical significance, did have the positive sign expected for it.

In the fertility regression, the coefficient of B was positive and significant. Except for wife's wage, which was negative but negligible in its impact on family size, all other coefficients were significant and had expected signs. Thus, in contrast to Cain & Dooley, fertility was negatively correlated with education. Of greater importance, however, was the negative and quite significant ($t=-8.5$) coefficient of the product, WMQ. This seems to support the authors' belief that quality is time intensive relative to alternatives to children.

Except for the coefficient of husband's wage, all other factors in the child quality regression were insignificant.

Some interesting findings are obtained in the regression

for wife's labor supply. Specifically, the coefficient of
family size is positive (unexpected), while that of child
quality is negative (expected). Both are marginally significant. While this supports the supposition that it is Q rather
than N that is the more time intensive, such a conclusion is
contrary to my own findings (Chapter 6). Of equal interest,
moreover, is the negative coefficient of wife's education,
although the latter is just barely significant (t=-1.7). A-
gain, this compares somewhat with the insignificant education
coefficient obtained by Cain & Dooley. Beyond these observations, all other coefficients are significant and with expected signs.

Upon comparison of the Cain-Dooley model with that of
Fleisher & Rhodes, the following observations are noted. First,
in the labor supply estimates, both models agree on the positive impact of wife's wage rate, and the negative effect of husband's income. Similarly, in each fertility regression the coefficients of wife's wage and husband's income are negative and
positive respectively. Thus, both models imply a strong substitution effect on the demand for numbers of children and the
supply of wife's labor, given a change in wife's earning power.
Finally, both models support the expectation that an increase
in wife's schooling tends to raise her expected wage, although
there is disagreement about the effect on labor force participation here. Quite probably, this latter contradiction is attributable to the inclusion of a demand variable (i.e., indus-

try mix) by Cain & Dooley.  No such provision was made by
Fleisher & Rhodes.

# 4. THE BASIC MODEL

Having reviewed the literature on the subject, I now proceed to construct and test a model of fertility behavior of my own.

By way of procedure, the first task is to formulate a Becker-type problem of constrained welfare maximization in which the demands for numbers of children, child premium (similar to Becker's 'child quality), and living standard are calculated to be functions of wife's wage and husband's income.

Having dealt with income variables, the next step involves the integration of a set of socioeconomic factors into the fabric of the model. Here, I consider possible roles for family status, urbanization, parents' education, and fecundity time in the constraint of the maximization problem, as well as in the utility function itself. Also discussed is the case in which those factors affecting household behavior are of a stochastic nature. Thus, the signs of various income, substitution, 'utility substitution' (defined below), and risk effects are deduced, and a set of testable hypotheses assembled.

## THE MODEL WITH INCOME VARIABLES ONLY

General Observations: As stated earlier, I expect to make use of those basic techniques of household production developed by Becker, and discussed at length in Chapter 3. Specifically, utility is to be derived from alternative commodities, the production of which requires inputs of market goods and home time. Consequently, any change in the relative prices of these inputs (i.e., the real wage) generates positive income effects on the demands for all commodities. Substitution effects, on the other hand, are positive for goods-intensive, and negative for time-intensive commodities. Thus, the demand for the former moves in the same direction as the change in the real wage, while the change in demand for the latter depends on which of the positive income or negative substitution effects has the greater magnitude.

To illustrate the point just made, identify commodities $Z_i$ and $Z_j$ in Figure 3-1 as 'child services' and 'living standard' respectively. Now, if the production of the former is time intensive relative to that of the latter as illustrated ( and if Samuelson-Stolper conditions are met), it follows that an increase in the market value of time generates substitution and income effects which are reenforcing on the demand for living standard ($Z_j$), and offsetting on the demand for child services ($Z_i$). Thus, an econometric test of the effects of higher real wage rates on demands for the two commodities would have experimental hypotheses stating expectations of a positive influence on optimum living standard, and an uncertain influence on the optimum level of child services.

While it is my intention to use a specification similar to that just outlined, I also follow the tradition of including, in addition to child services (taken here to vary directly with numbers of children) and living standard, a third argument in the utility function, i.e., 'child premium' to be defined below. The resulting solution to the constrained maximization problem thus yields, given changes in either parent's income potential, functions not only for the demand for numbers of children, but also for various goods and services optimum levels of which are influenced by family size.

The Utility Function: Accepting Willis' reply to Samuelson's observations regarding welfare functions (Chapter 1), I begin by specifying a utility function for parents. The arguments of this function are:

'Numbers of Children' (C): This designates the number of offspring that parents choose to bear and raise to maturity over the remainder of the household's fecundity. While questions such as the spacing of a given number of children are frequently as important as the number itself, my discussion of the problem of maximization over time (below) is brief, the greater part of my efforts being concentrated on family size alone.

'Child Premium' (P): In Chapter 3, treatments by Becker, et al of the quality aspect of children were discussed. Similarly, I use the term 'child premium' to designate those allocations of goods and time designed to raise the total utility of a specific number of children. Stated alternatively, child premium stands for those commodities for which the cross-partial of total utility between numbers of children and premium itself (i.e., $U_{cp}$) is positive, although small enough to insure the maintenance of second-order maximization conditions. While the distinction is not developed exhaustively, it might be noted in passing that P itself can be subdivided into (a) those items

for which marginal utility is positive only if C exceeds zero, i.e., various toys, nursery paraphernalia, children's
schooling, etc., and (b) commodities capable of providing satisfaction to parents even with the absence of children, i.e.,
housing, some types of travel, etc.

Before leaving this point, a word on my rationale for using 'child premium' rather than 'child quality' is in order.
Specifically, Becker has incorporated into his most recent models (1973, 1981, see Chapter 3) a quantity-quality interaction
within the constraint of the maximization problem. While I accept the possibility that such an interaction exists, I have
decided to weave it into the utility function instead. This is
because I consider the variety of forms such an interaction
might assume to be as great as the variety of individual family
idiosyncracies vis-a-vis fertility behavior, and not confined to
the number of alternative specifications of the constraint,
which I consider to be more limited. Thus, were I to have dealt
with a quantity-quality interaction through modification of the
constraint (a la Becker), then the term 'child quality' would
have been apropos.

'Living Standard' (S): This argument can be thought of
as the strict alternative to child services since it includes
all commodities whose role in the utility function is independent of numbers of children. I also assume that the effect of
S within the utility function is independent of P. While this
facilitates the calculation of substitution and income effects

later on, there exists a good economic justification for such an assumption.[1] If two commodities, X and Y are perfect substitutes, then the cross partial, Uxy, is negative and equal in magnitude to either second partial, i.e., Uxx or Uyy. This indicates that X and Y are equally adaptable to the attainment of a type of satisfaction whose nature is very narrowly defined. Consequently, the acquisition of one more unit of Y would have, assuming equal unit prices, the same effect on the marginal utility of X as would have been the case had one more unit of X been obtained instead. As the nature of the satisfaction gotten from X and Y becomes more general, then, the absolute value of Uxy falls. At the extreme of generality, therefore, X and Y perform services that are totally independent, and they are separable within the utility function, so that Uxy is zero. It is assumed here that C and P, on one hand, and S on the other, exemplify this extreme.

The Form of the Utility Function:  Given the nature of its arguments, the utility function takes the following general form:

$$U = U(\emptyset(C,P),S)$$

...where $\emptyset(C,P)$ indicates the unique relationship between numbers of children and child premium, as well as the separability of the latter commodities from living standard. Given non-

---

[1] To make the distinction between P and S less abstract, consider as examples of S such commodities as luxury foods, furs and jewelry not intended to be passed on to children, sports cars (as opposed to station wagons), evening entertainment at or travel to places not suited to children, etc.

satiation and diminishing marginal utility, therefore, we have:

$$U\emptyset s = Ucs = Ups = 0$$
$$U\emptyset > 0 \qquad \emptyset c > 0 \qquad \emptyset p > 0$$
$$U\emptyset\emptyset < 0 \qquad \emptyset cp > 0$$

In addition, one could specify non-positive values for $\emptyset cc$ and $\emptyset pp$ as sufficient conditions for diminishing marginal utility, although all that is necessary here is for $Ucc$ and $Upp$ to be negative.[2]

The Constraint: In this model, I assume that one of the parents (traditionally the husband) has a comparative advantage in generating income from participation in the labor market. While the other parent may be active here as well, that individual's comparative advantage lies with domestic productive activity, i.e., providing the time inputs required for C and P, as well as joining with other family members in the contribution of time for living standard.[3] Thus, this might be classified as a 'Passive Husband Model'.

As in the more simple model without child premium, maximization of the utility function is constrained by husband's and other income (Y), plus the market value of wife's available time (WT); where as before, 'W' is wife's real wage rate, and 'T' is the total number of time (or wage) periods available over the remainder of the household's fecundity.

[2] A specific example is: $U = G((g_1 + g_2(P/C)^b)C^a + g_3 P^{b'} + g_4 S^c)$
...where all exponents have values between zero and one. The additivity property, however, may not be necessary.

[3] See Becker (1981, Chapter 2) for a discussion of comparative advantage within the household.

Unlike Becker, I permit W and T to assume scaler rather than vector values. While Becker's argument with respect to the multidimensionality of time is well taken, I believe this question can be circumvented by having each of the wage units in T be long enough to contain representative proportions of all time dimensions.

A quantity of children, C, is maintained with inputs of time, t, in wage periods, and goods and services, h, obtained from the marketplace. Thus, the production function is written:

$$C = C(h,t)$$

At this point, the model can go in either of two directions. If, for example, the household can acquire domestic services, then variable proportions could be permitted in the production function for numbers of children. This is because such services, while performing the function of time, are bought in the marketplace, and must thus be classified among those items referred to as goods. Should the production function exhibit constant returns to scale, moreover, we could then write the cost function for children as X(W)C, where X(W) is average cost per child assuming that optimum factor proportions are always used. Note that since the decision time required to alter factor proportions is the same for both time and goods, there is no Marshallean Short Run per se. Thus, X(W) represents the cost associated with obtaining, given W, the optimum factor combination. Observation suggests, however, that the production function for numbers of children is subject to increasing returns to scale. While more is said about this point and its implications for child spacing strategy, below, I do not think that the basic model presented here is so abstract as to exclude so obvious an aspect of reality. Consequently, I express the cost function for numbers of children as $X(C,W)$, where $X_c$ is positive, and $X_{cc}$ is negative. Observe at this point an advantage to the incorporation of the quantity-quality interaction into the utility function rather than the constraint. Specifically, I may recognize the existence of this interaction without having to introduce, as does Becker (see Chapter 3), seperate terms defining fixed and variable costs of child service production. I am, however, obliged to make special arrangements for the incorporation of socioeconomic factors into the model (below). Becker, it will be recalled, chose to make the quantity-quality interaction a focal point for discussion of the effects of the latter variables. Since socioeconomic factors are usually addressed in the context of the constraint (see DeTray & Michael, Chapter 3), his specification of the interaction there made it possible for him to do so.

An alternative assumption would be that domestic services are not widely available (or are too costly to warrant consideration by the household). In this case, it is appropriate to assume that the production of unappreciated (i.e., $P=0$) children requires some minimum inputs of both goods and time, and that these minima occur in some fixed proportion. Thus with

constant returns to scale, the total cost of maintaining children, $X(C,W)$, is equal to $(Wt+h)C$, where 't' and 'h' are those
minimum requirements of time and goods per child respectively;
while the recognition of increasing returns to scale would have
us write $X(C,W) = (Wt(C) = h(C))$, should the fixed factor proportions depend on the magnitude of C, or $X(C,W) = (Wt+h)f(C)$,
where fc is positive and fcc is negative, should the required
ratio of goods to time not be affected by C. Fortunately,
whichever case is used, Xc and Xcc are positive and negative respectively given increasing returns to scale.

The point just made has more than mere pedantic importance.
Recall that child rearing is assumed to be relatively time intensive. Should variable proportions be permitted within a
Cobb-Douglas production function for numbers of children, then
the latter assumption can be realized by merely making the ex-
ponent of time relative to that of goods greater than the ratio
of these exponents within the production functions for child
premium and living standard, where variable proportions most
definitely exist. With fixed proportions in the production
function for children, and variable proportions in the production functions for the other commodities, however, an obvious
problem arises. Specifically, it is possible for W to be so
low that the chosen time intensity for S is greater than the required time intensity for C. Should fixed proportions be used
in producing the latter, therefore, it would be necessary to
assume that the value of W for which living standard and child

premium become more time intensive than child rearing is less than that value of W just sufficient to induce the wife to supply labor in the marketplace.

Child premium and living standard are also produced with inputs of goods and time. In their cases, however, I only consider the possibility of variable proportions. At this point, the possibility of joint production must be recognized. I believe, however, that this possibility can be ignored since the frequency of its occurance is probably less than one might expect at first glance. Specifically, there can be no joint production attainable from inputs allocated to the production of C since goods and time used for that end are the absolute minima needed. Thus, by definition, there can be no amount of P obtained from their use in C production. If these inputs are highly specialized, moreover, then joint production of S is also precluded. With respect to the possibility of joint production between P and S, it is true that a given commodity might be capable of generating both of these simultaneously. I shall assume, however, that the household has the option either to avail itself of a dual usage of this sort, or to allocate the products of goods and time to either P or S exclusively. I assume further that the dual allocation serves to increase the rate of depreciation of goods and/or to reduce the productivity of time to such an extent that the classic benefits of joint production are eliminated. Thus, while a rigorous treatment of joint production in the household is provided by Grossman (1971), I shall not consider it in the formulation of my own basic model.

Finally, I recognize the probability of increasing returns to scale in the production of child premium and living standard. Therefore, expenditures for these latter arguments together can be expressed as $J(W,P) + K(W,S)$, where Jp and Ks are positive, Jpp and Kss are negative, and Jw, Jpw, Kw, and Ksw are all positive.

In summary, then, the objective is to:

$$\text{Maximize } U = U(C,P,S)$$
$$\text{Subject to } WT + Y = X(W,C) + J(W,P) + K(W,S)$$

The Effects of Changes in Income Variables: After having determined first and second order maximization conditions, the demand functions for numbers of children, child premium, and living standard may be outlined (see Appendix). Given the marginal utility of income, $\lambda$, it is sufficient for second order conditions to hold if (1) $(Ucc-\lambda Xcc)$, $(Upp-\lambda Jpp)$, and $(Uss-\lambda Kss)$, hereafter abbreviated as $Ucc'$, $Upp'$, and $Uss'$ respectively, are all negative. In other words, the rate of decline in any marginal utility is greater than the marginal utility to be derived from any scale economies within the production function for that commodity. And (2), the arguments of the utility function must be gross substitutes, a condition recognized earlier by having (a) S be independent of C and P in the utility function (i.e., $Ucs=Ups=0$), and (b) the net rate of decline in the marginal utility of C or P (i.e., $Ucc'$ and $Upp'$) be greater than the rate of increase in the marginal utility of C (or P) given increases in P (or C) (see Appendix).

With a change in wife's wage (W), substitution and income effects are generated on the demands for C, P, and S. These are summarized in Table 4-1. Given the two assumptions just outlined, three arguments in the utility function imply a Bordered Hessian whose determinant, D, is negative. Thus, $-D$ $(=Uss'Jp^2-2UcpXcJp+Upp'Xc^2)+Ks^2(Ucc'Upp'-Ucp^2))$ is positive so that the sign of the substitution effect is the same as that of the numerator.

Table 4-1

Effects of Changes in Wife's Wage

| | SUBSTITUTION EFFECT | INCOME EFFECT |
|---|---|---|
| $\partial C/\partial W$: | $\lambda\dfrac{Uss'Jp(XcwJp-JpwXc)}{-D}$ | $\dfrac{(T+L')Uss'(Upp'Xc-UcpJp)}{-D}$ |
| | $+\ \lambda\dfrac{Upp'Ks(KsXcw-KswXc)}{-D}$ | |
| | $+\ \lambda\dfrac{UcpKs(KswJp-KsJpw)}{-D}$ | |
| $\partial P/\partial W$: | $\lambda\dfrac{Uss'Xc(XcJpw-XcwJp)}{-D}$ | $\dfrac{(T+L')Uss'(Ucc'Jp-UcpXc)}{-D}$ |
| | $+\ \lambda\dfrac{Ucc'Ks(KsJpw-JpKsw)}{-D}$ | |
| | $+\ \lambda\dfrac{UcpKs(XcKsw-KsXcw)}{-D}$ | |
| $\partial S/\partial W$: | $\lambda\dfrac{Ucc'Jp(KswJp-KsJpw)}{-D}$ | $\dfrac{(T+L')Ks(Upp'Ucc'-Ucp^2)}{-D}$ |
| | $+\ \lambda\dfrac{Upp'Xc(KswXc-KsXcw)}{-D}$ | |
| | $+\ \lambda\dfrac{Ucp(Xc(KsJpw-KswJp)+Jp(KsXcw-KswXc))}{-D}$ | |

Examining first the substitution effects, a good strategy for determining signs is to divide terms in parentheses by those marginal cost factors contained within them, i.e., Xc,

Jp, and Ks. Since this operation results in differences in proportional changes in marginal costs given changes in wife's wage (i.e., Xcw/Xc, Jpw/Jp, and Ksw/Ks), assumptions about relative time intensities can then be employed to deduce substitution effect elements as being either positive or negative.

Using recent literature as a guide, I propose the assumption that C production is the most time intensive, S production the least time intensive, and that the production of P be of a time intensity that takes the middle position. It follows, then, that the rank of proportional changes in marginal costs of commodities given a change in W is the same as the hierarchy of time intensities.[4]

Armed with the assumptions just stated, and given previous stipulations about the signs of Ucc', Upp', Uss', and Ucp, it is clear that the substitution effect from changes in wife's wage is negative on the demand for numbers of children, positive on the demand for living standard, and of either sign with respect to the demand for child premium.

---

[4]Samuelson-Stolper conditions are sufficient for this conclusion to be made. While I am willing to accept the latter two of these conditions, i.e., those establishing a constant ordering of different factor intensities over the entire range of factor price ratios, I hesitate to assume linear homogeneity because of the likelihood of scale economies. Instead, I make the weaker assumption that production functions are homothetic, and that any scenario in which the absence of linear homogeneity could bring about a factor intensity reversal given a change in W is of trivial significance. Before leaving this point, it might be noted that the presence of scale economies has an additional cost of preempting use of the less complicated 'dual' procedure in determining various demand curves. See: Henderson & Quandt (1980) pp. 41-44.

Within the income effects, L' is the change in wife's labor supply resulting from a change in her real wage, and is equal to $-(X_w+J_w+K_w)$. While this value may itself be of either sign, the term, $(T+L')$, must be positive, total time being greater than the change in time supplied to the labor market. Consequently, all income effects are positive. Here, it can also be noted that, given the passive husband nature of my model, a change in husband's income (Y) can also be counted upon to have a positive effect on the demands for all three commodities. Specifically, the effect of a change in Y is the same as the income effects arising from a change in W with the exception that, in the former case, the term, $(T+L')$, is replaced by unity.

Other Observations: In addition to conclusions drawn about the signs of substitution and income effects given changes in W and/or Y, a number of other observations can be made.

First, observe that as $U_{ss'}$ approaches zero, the income effect disappears, while the substitution effect retains some negative value. This point is explored further below.

A second observation involves the marginal utility of income, $\lambda$, which is expected to fall as husband's and/or asset income increases. Thus, should satiation with income occur, substitution effects would disappear, and $\partial C/\partial W$ would assume the positive value of the income effect.

Recalling Adelman's findings (Chapter 2), which my own investigations seem to support (Chapters 5 & 6), that economic development tends to reduce the total impact of income variables on fertility, it would appear that a reduction in the rate of decline in Us accompanies such progress. Combined with the obvious effect of development on income, then, the reduction in income and substitution effects implied by the latter two observations appears to have empirical support. These relationships are examined further in the discussion of socioeconomic factors below.

Maximization Over Time: Since I am concerned about the long-run question of completed family size, I believe it satisfactory here to make only a brief digression to the more short-run problem of child-spacing strategy.

To begin, the utility function is rewritten:

$$U = U(C_1, C_2, \ldots, C_F; P_1, P_2, \ldots, P_F; S_1, S_2, \ldots, S_F)$$

...where $C_i$, $P_i$, and $S_i$ are acquisitions of new children, child premium, and living standard during the $i^{th}$ period after the formation of the household. The utility function applies over the household's lifetime, i.e., a span of F periods.[5]

The utility function is then maximized subject to the constraint of discounted full family wealth, i.e.,

$$\sum_{i=1}^{F} \frac{W_i T + Y_i}{(1+r)^i} = \sum_{i=1}^{F} \left\{ \left[ X_i(W_i; C_1, C_2, \ldots, C_i; P_1, P_2, \ldots, P_i) \right. \right.$$
$$\left. \left. + J_i(W_i; P_1, P_2, \ldots, P_i) + K_i(W_i; S_1, S_2, \ldots, S_i) \right] / (1+r)^i \right\}$$

Here, 'r' is the rate of discount, and 'T' is time available

[5]So that problems of discontinuity related to the indivisibility of children may be minimized, let each period be long enough (perhaps five years) to permit the bearing of more than one child.

per period. Observe that the cost of raising children born during period 'i' is affected by expenditures on premium made during periods leading up to and including 'i'.

Next, first-order maximization conditions may be determined, and an optimum MRS between $C_j$ and $C_k$ defined, i.e.,

$$U_{C_j}/U_{C_k} = \sum_{i=j}^{F} (\frac{\partial X_i}{\partial C_j} \frac{1}{(1+r)^i}) / \sum_{i=k}^{F} (\frac{\partial X_i}{\partial C_k} \frac{1}{(1+r)^i})$$

A number of observations relating these first-order conditions to the question of child spacing can now be made.

First, in the case of the utility function (and therefore, the MRS), it seems probable that, with a specific number of children, satisfaction is greater the farther apart births are spaced. The rationale here is clear. As a child matures, the nature of the utility obtained by parents from his presence changes. In other words, a different kind of satisfaction is derived from an infant as opposed to a school-aged child, an adolescent, etc. Now, if births are closely spaced, then the quantity of children at any given stage of maturity is greater than would have been the case had births been more evenly spaced throughout the household's fecundity. Thus, total satisfaction is less given, say three adolescents, than perhaps one high-schooler, one grade-schooler, and one pre-schooler. Moreover, with a spacing that is more distant among births, parents can get some measure of utility from the presence of children over a greater length of time. I assume here, of course, that child rearing does not extend so far into parents' lifetimes as to create a significant inconvenience.

With respect to the ratio of shadow prices, the child spacing strategy selected can have two offsetting effects vis-a-vis the presence of scale economies in child service production. First, it seems probable that the total cost of a given number of children is less if children are more closely spaced. This is because inputs of goods and time uniquely required by a single child of a particular age need not be doubled in order to support a second child of approximately the same age. Were these children to have been more distantly spaced, on the other hand, it is likely that many inputs devoted to the older child could not have been of immediate use in raising the younger.

Alternatively, it appears that the time intensity of child rearing declines as children become older. Thus, if children were spaced farther apart in time, the loss of those scale economies identified with closer spacing becomes compensated to some extent by the ability of older children to contribute a portion to the time input needed for the raising of younger children.

Thus, with a specific number of children, there is a utility effect encouraging parents to space births more evenly throughout their fecundity. Also encouraging a greater variance on children's ages is the saving of mother's time should older children be able to care for their younger siblings. Offsetting these, however, is the greater efficiency with which both goods and time can be used should births be more concentrated in time. It follows, then, that a proper spacing strategy must have as its objective the equating of the marginal utility resulting from a more protracted interval between births with the marginal cost of any net reduction in economies of scale.

THE INCORPORATION OF NON-INCOME VARIABLES

I am now ready to integrate into the model just presented a number of those non-income or socioeconomic variables which the literature has shown to be instrumental in determining fertility behavior. Having reviewed this literature from both the Easterlin and Becker perspectives, I have selected five factors generally recognized as being of importance. These are: urbanization, parents' education, age of marriage and divorce probability, social status, and child mortality. The task at hand is complicated because there are three ways by which these variables might exercise their influences. First, socioeconomic factors may have an impact on the constraint of the maximization problem via their effect on the net cost of raising children. Second, these factors may make their influence felt within the utility function itself, specifically by affecting the marginal utilities of one or more of the arguments of that function. Finally, there is the possibility that a stochastic term could be generated. This latter effect, moreover, is further complicated by the likelihood that the variance of the latter term could, in addition to its mean, affect the solution to the maximization problem should a propensity for risk avoidance or acceptance be implied by parents' preferences.

By way of procedure, then, I shall examine in turn each of these manifestations of the relevant socioeconomic factors.

Socioeconomic Factors and the Constraint: When considering possible modifications to the constraint, I focus attention primarily on the effects of urbanization, parents' education, and age of marriage and divorce probability.

Urbanization: In the previous two chapters, we saw that most of the studies designed to determine the effect of socio-economic variables on fertility recognized the role of urbaniza-tion and/or industrialization. Except for Adelman, moreover, all authors pointed out how the net cost of children tends to be greater in urban than in rural areas. Specifically, should we assume that an agricultural enterprise is normally organized as a family proprietorship, it is then possible, keeping DeTray's warnings (Chapter 3) in mind, that in rural areas, children are in a better position to contribute to family income than they would be in an urban setting, where child labor legislation for example would magnify the difficulty of their finding employment outside any family concern. Using population density to repre-sent the degree of urbanization, I specify a function, $m=m(R,C)$; where 'm' is the real augmentation of income from numbers of children (C), and 'R' is population per square mile. Assuming diminishing marginal productivity, and that child productivity falls asymptotically with urbanization, I also specify that $m_c$ and $m_{RR}$ are positive, while $m_{cR}$, $m_{cc}$, and $m_R$ are all negative.

The original constraint is then rewritten:

$$WT + Y = X(C,W) + J(P,W) + K(S,W) - m(R,C)$$

Differentiating first-order conditions with respect to R (see Appendix), substitution and income effects from changes in urbanization can then be deduced. These are summarized in Table 4-2. Here, $Ucc"$ is equal to $Ucc - \lambda(Xcc - m_{cc})$, while $D'$ is essentially the same as D with the exception that $Ucc"$ replaces $Ucc'$ in its calculation.

Table 4-2

Effects of Urbanization

|  | SUBSTITUTION EFFECT | INCOME EFFECT |
|---|---|---|
| $\frac{\partial C}{\partial R}$: | $\dfrac{-\lambda m_{cR}(Ks^2 Upp' + Jp^2 Uss')}{-D'}$ | $\dfrac{m_R Uss'(Upp'Xc - UcpJp)}{-D'}$ |
| $\frac{\partial P}{\partial R}$: | $\dfrac{\lambda m_{cR}(UcpKs^2 + XcJpUss')}{-D'}$ | $\dfrac{-m_R Uss'(UcpXc - Ucc"Jp)}{-D'}$ |
| $\frac{\partial S}{\partial R}$: | $\dfrac{\lambda m_{cR}(Upp'Xc - UcpJp)}{-D'}$ | $\dfrac{m_R Ks(Ucc"Upp' - Ucp^2)}{-D'}$ |

As might be expected, all income effects are negative, reflecting the detrimental effect of R on children's earning abilities. Similarly, the substitution effects on demands for C and S are negative and positive respectively, while the compensated change in optimum P from increased R can assume either sign, a positive value becoming more likely as the marginal cost of numbers of children (Xc) increases.

Observe that the negative $m_{cc}$, i.e., the rate of change in the marginal income earning potential of children, tends to offset Xcc, i.e., the rate of increase in the marginal cost of children, also a negative value given the assumption of scale economies. Thus, the absolute value of Ucc" is greater than that of Ucc', and in turn, -D' is greater than -D. This is important because it suggests an interaction between urbanization and the effects of income variables, W and Y, on fertility. To develop this point, a re-inspection of the substitution and income effects generated by a change in wife's wage suggests a diminution in the absolute values of both given -D' rather than -D. While the resulting change in $\partial C/\partial W$ cannot always be predicted a priori since substitution and income effects are offsetting, there should be a clear reduction in $\partial C/\partial Y$, were -D' to be used rather than -D. Now, should I stipulate that urbanization tends to reduce not only the absolute value of $m_c$, but also that of $m_{cc}$, then it could be shown that:

$$(\partial C/\partial Y)/ R > 0$$

Thus, if the effects of urbanization are confined exclusively to the constraint, a greater value of R should serve to raise the effect of changes in husband's income on intended family size.

Parents' Education: In considering the effect of parents' education as a consumer good, I suggest, in the spirit of Michael and DeTray (Chapter 3), that it be incorporated as a technological factor in the production functions for one or more of C, P, and S. Thus, if we specify expenditure functions $X(C,W,E)$, $J(P,W,E)$, and $K(S,W,E)$, where $X_E$, $J_E$, and $K_E$ are all negative implying a reduction in total cost given an increase in education; and $X_{CE}$, $J_{PE}$, and $K_{SE}$ are also negative suggest-

ing a reduction in marginal costs as well, substitution and income effects resulting from a change in E can then be calculated. Actually, these need not be set down here in detail
since their general format is exactly the same as those of
$\partial C/\partial W$, $\partial P/\partial W$, and $\partial S/\partial W$, with two exceptions. These are (a)
the positive Xcw, Ksw, and Jpw are replaced by the negative
$X_{CE}$, $J_{PE}$, and $K_{SE}$, and (b) the term, (T+L'), in each of the income effects is replaced by $(-)(K_E+J_E)$. Clearly then, all income effects are positive as expected, a higher level of
utility being realized from a given amount of goods and time.
The substitution effects, however, offer an area of greater interest. Should education affect household technology in a way
that is 'goods using', as suggested by DeTray, for example,
then the reduction in marginal costs of premium and living standard would exceed the reduction in the cost of an additional
child, again causing the demand for the latter to fall (at
least so far as the substitution effect is concerned) as consumption education rises. Thus, the effect of parents' education on fertility depends on which of the offsetting substitution and income effects is the stronger. The likelihood of
the former having the greater magnitude, moreover, varies directly with the relative time intensity of child rearing.

Finally, there is an interaction between parents' education and urbanization that is quite similar to that identified
between urbanization and wife's real wage. Just as the latter
was of an uncertain direction because of offsetting substitu-

tion and income effects, however, the interaction resulting from the effect of urbanization on $\partial C/\partial E$ is similarly indefinite.

Fecundity Time: Here, two factors present themselves as having importance, i.e., age of marriage and probability of divorce. Since an increase in either of these elements results in a reduction in T (i.e., total wage periods in the household's fecundity), it follows that such an increase creates a negative income effect on optimum levels of all arguments in the utility function.

Socioeconomic Factors and the Utility Function: As suggested by Michael, economists have tended to shy away from the development of a theory of preference formation. While the justification for this can probably be traced to and supported by Stanley Jevons' demonstration of the non-existence of a 'community utility function', it may nevertheless be possible to predict (without resorting to a cardinal concept of utility) the aggregate effect of a change in some independent variable on tastes by showing that changes in that variable tend to move the structures of individual utility functions in a common direction.

To illustrate the latter point, consider the fundamental model of constrained utility maximization, i.e., maximize $U = U(X,Y)$ subject to $I = P_xX + P_yY$. I stipulate, however, that $U_x$ is a function of some socioeconomic, non-price parameter, Z, such that $U_{xz}$ is positive for all individuals in the community. Now, proceeding to determine first and second order conditions for utility maximization, I obtain:

$$\frac{\partial X}{\partial Z} = \frac{UxzPy^2}{D} \quad \text{and} \quad \frac{\partial Y}{\partial Z} = \frac{-UxzPxPy}{D}$$

where 'D', the determinant of the matrix of partial derivatives of first-order conditions, is positive. Clearly, this is a rather elegant way to state the obvious, i.e., that any factor which enhances the marginal utility of either of the arguments of the utility function makes that commodity more desirable, and the alternative commodity less so. I choose to call this a 'Utility Substitution Effect'. While there is nothing particularly outstanding about this observation, it is nevertheless clear that the identification of a social factor such as 'Z' would enable us to make predictions every bit as reliable as those which economists have traditionally made regarding changes in price and income variables. There is more. Should some 'Z' have a positive influence on the marginal utility of at least one good, and a non-negative effect on the marginal utilities of all other goods, it follows that the individual's condition (i.e., maximum total utility) improves with an increase in the value of Z. While this might be called a 'Utility Income Effect', it differs in one very important way from the traditional income effect. Specifically, with the latter, one notes a decline in the marginal utility of income ($\lambda$). Calculating $\partial\lambda/\partial Z$, however:

$$\frac{\partial \lambda}{\partial Z} = \frac{Uxz(UxyPy - UyyPx)}{D}$$

...we have a value that is clearly positive. While this utility income effect does not influence optimum X and Y per se, it does have some rather important implications so far as labor force participation is concerned. Clearly, the decline in $\lambda$ implied by the traditional income effect suggests a decline in labor time given a constant real wage. Conversely then, the increases in the marginal utility of income resulting from this effect would point to an increase in labor supply. While this point is revisited briefly in Chapter 6, the task here is to examine those socioeconomic factors capable of generating utility substitution effects. The two variables that immediately come to mind in this context are urbanization and status, the latter to be reflected in intended living standard.

Urbanization: Earlier, while discussing the income effect of a change in wife's real wage on optimum number of children, it was noted that a dominance of the substitution effect here becomes more likely if Us (i.e., the marginal utility of living standard) falls more slowly. Furthermore, it was postulated that satiation with living standard is less likely if there exists a greater variety of consumer goods available to the family. I believe I am on safe ground in assuming that the latter condition is more probable in an urban rather than a rural setting. Consequently, I expect Uss (and quite probably Upp) for a given family transplanted from a rural to an urban environment to decline in absolute value as the rural experience recedes into the past. Assuming therefore that Up and Us take on values in

98

an urban setting for initial acquisitions of P and S at least
as great as those for a rural residence, it follows from the
slower rates of decline in these marginal utilities from urbanization that $U_{pR}$ and $U_{sR}$ rise with R. Consequently, there
is a utility substitution effect that is definitely positive
for living standard, definitely negative for numbers of children, and uncertain for child premium, average premium probably
rising, but the decline in number of children tending to reduce
total premium. The total effect of urbanization on fertility
can thus be augmented to include (a) the substitution effect
(i.e., the form of the utility function and the level of total
utility are constant), (b) the income effect (relative net
costs are constant), and (c) the utility substitution effect.
This is illustrated in Figure 4-1. Here, the original value of

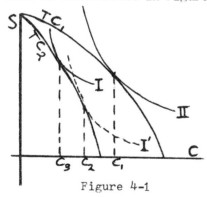

R implies optimum C and S (P
is eliminated for simplicity)
at the tangency of transformation curve II, i.e., at $C_1$, $S_1$.
Given an increase in R, TC
shifts to $TC_2$ whose steeper
slope reflects the specification
that lost family income from ur-

Figure 4-1

banization varies directly with the level of C. Now, if there
were to be no utility substitution effect, then C falls from $C_1$
to $C_2$, i.e., at the tangency of $TC_2$ and indifference curve I'.
With the presence of the utility substitution effect as des-

cribed, however, the indifference map shifts, so that the tangency is now between $TC_2$ and indifference curve I, i.e., at $C=C_3$.

Status: In considering the effect of status on fertility I follow the lead of Easterlin (Chapter 2), associating that factor with intended consumption as represented by grandparents' income (V). Now, if a greater level of consumption is postulated to be enjoyed by parents while they were still part of their own parents' households, then a retardation in the rate of approach to satiation with living standard is expected, i.e., increases in V serve to reduce the absolute value of $U_{ss}$. Consequently, the utility effect of V on fertility is negative as was the case with urbanization.

Before leaving this point, it might be useful to recall the relationship between $U_{ss}$ and $\partial C/\partial Y$, and the income effect of $\partial C/\partial W$ discussed earlier. Specifically, as $U_{ss}$ approaches zero, so too do both of the latter. Thus, an increased value of V suggests a reduction in the responsiveness of fertility to changes in family income. While its specification within the utility function points to the same phenomenon given increased urbanization, it should be remembered that the effect of R within the constraint tends to raise the responsiveness of family size to changes in family income.

Stochastic Terms and the Utility Function: While my own econometric tests using regions of a developed society (Chapters 5 & 6) lead me to ignore those risk factors discussed in the literature, a few observations on stochastic terms can be stated here.

To begin an analysis of these factors, denote 'd' as the probability that any one child will not survive to maturity, and 'b' as a multiplier reflecting total births divided by the number of planned births expected to occur over the household's fecundity. I assume for the sake of simplicity that 'b' itself is not a function of the number of planned births. Thus, $C = Bb(1-d)$, where 'C' is total number of children as before, and 'B' is the number of planned births over the household's fecundity. Now, since each of b and d follows some distribution with means $\bar{b}$ and $\bar{d}$, and variances $\delta_b^2$ and $\delta_d^2$ respectively, the existence of a single distribution with mean, $\bar{b}(1-\bar{d})$, and variance $\delta^2$ can be imagined. The task facing the household, then, is to maximize Expected Utility, $E(U)$, with respect to B, where:

$$E(U) = \sum_{i=0}^{CM} r_i(B,b,d)U^*(C_i)$$

Here, '$r_i$' is the probability of $C_i$ children surviving to maturity given the number of intended births, B, and the combined b,d probability distribution; and $U^*(C_i)$ is maximum possible utility given $C_i$ children raised to maturity, i.e., that level of satisfaction achieved with optimum P and S when $C=C_i$. 'CM' is the maximum possible number of children that could be raised to maturity over the lifetime of the household. The question thus involves conditions for which $E(U)$ is or is not maximized at a value of B such that the household expects to have the same

number of surviving children as was the case with the non-
stochastic model, i.e., 'i' is such that $U^*(C_i)$ is itself
maximized. Concerning this point, consider the following observations.[6]

First, if parents perceive the loss in utility resulting
from a given number of children less than $C^*$ (i.e., that 'C'
which maximizes U) to be equal to that of the same number of
children more than $C^*$, i.e., are 'risk-neutral', then B =
$C^*/\bar{b}(1-\bar{d})$, regardless of the magnitude of $\delta^2$.

Secondly, if parents have a bias against fewer or more
than the optimum number of offspring, then of course, they
would seek to 'insure' against the 'greater evil' by setting
B equal to a value that increases the probability of the 'lesser
evil'. Moreover, the degree of 'insurance' sought varies directly with $\delta^2$. For example, if this variance is zero, then
no insurance is needed since C as a function of B, b, and d is
not stochastic. Similarly, as $\delta^2$ increases, then so too does
the risk associated with the 'greater evil'.

Given these observations, then, it remains to determine
the effect on $\delta^2$ of changes in family income, urbanization,
and parents' education.

Letting 'Y' serve as an indicator of family income, and
assuming (a) that Y and child mortality, d, are inversely related, and (b) that d and $\delta^2$ are directly related (i.e., if d
follows a Binomial Distribution, then $\bar{d}$ is assumed to be less

---

[6] For a discussion of utility maximization under conditions of
uncertainty, see Henderson & Quandt (1980) pp. 56-60.

than 0.5); it follows that increases in Y cause intended
births, B, to be adjusted so that the optimum number of children expected to survive to maturity converges to C*. In other
words, $\partial \delta^2 / \partial Y$ is augmented by the term, $(\partial C / \partial \delta^2)(\partial \delta^2 / \partial Y)$, reflecting the degree to which optimum C is affected by the in-
fluence of income on the risk associated with failure to a-
chieve C*. This term can be of either sign. Clearly, the assumption about the relationship between Y and $\delta^2$ suggests that
$\partial \delta^2 / \partial Y$ is negative. The sign of $\partial C / \partial \delta^2$, however, depends on
attitudes vis-a-vis the risk of over or underachievement of
optimum C. Specifically, a willingness to accept a greater
than optimum family size so as to insure against less than C*
means that the latter derivative is positive. By the same to-
ken, therefore, a negative value for $\partial C / \partial \delta^2$ implies a number
of offspring greater than C* is the greater evil. Consequently,
I expect that, ceteris paribus, $\partial C / \partial Y$ tends to be greater in
societies whose members prefer to insure against underachievement of P* and/or S*, than for societies whose members wish to
insure against fertility being less than optimum.

Following Michael's theoretical demonstration of how education can influence family size by exposing parents to a wider
array of contraceptive information, and keeping in mind the
observations made earlier (see Chapter 2) that the same could
be true for urbanization, it is clear that, as levels of parents' education and urbanization increase, the value of 'b'
approaches unity, and that $\delta^2$ is similarly reduced in value.

Thus, the risk effects within $\partial C/\partial E$ and $\partial C/\partial R$ are negative as was the case with $\partial C/\partial Y$.

SUMMARY

To summarize, then, it has been my objective here to examine the effects on fertility behavior of income variables, W and Y, as well as such socioeconomic factors as parents' education, urbanization, fecundity time, status, and child mortality. Having done this, two sets of experimental hypotheses may be constructed, i.e., those dealing with expected effects of independent variables per se, and those having to do with possible interactions among the effects of these variables on fertility. The first set of hypotheses is summarized in Table 4-3.

Table 4-3
Expected Effects on Optimum Fertility

| VARIABLE | EFFECTS ON FERTILITY | | | |
| --- | --- | --- | --- | --- |
| | SUBST. | INCOME | U.SUBST. | TOTAL |
| Status | | | - | - |
| Urbanization | - | - | - | - |
| Parents' Education | - | + | | - or + |
| Fecundity Time | + | | | + |
| Husband's Income | + | | | + |
| Wife's Wage | - | + | | - or + |

Since I conduct my empirical investigations using data from an economically developed society for which levels of income and education are relatively high (even in the least developed region), I have chosen to assume that risk effects are negligible.

With respect to various interactions, I give special attention to the influences of status (as represented by grandparents' income (V)), urbanization, and family income per se. To summarize, hypotheses made here include:

(1) As V increases, the effect on Uss serves to reduce all income effects on fertility. Recall that the latter are associated with husband's income, wife's wage, parents' education, urbanization, and grandparents' income itself.

(2) As R increases, offsetting interactions occur. First, the reduction in the absolute value of Uss causes interactions similar to those outlined in point (1), above. A higher degree of urbanization, however, also tends to lower the absolute value of $m_{cc}$ (see above) in the constraint. This suggests a magnification of all income effects on optimum number of children.

(3) Finally, any positive change in real income tends, ceteris paribus, to reduce the marginal utility of income. Thus, all substitution effects are reduced in magnitude.

As a general hypothesis, then, the tendency for status, urbanization, education, and income variables to move in a common direction with economic development leads me to expect that, for more developed regions, regression equations designed to test fertility behavior would have coefficients for the latter set of independent variables that are less significant statistically than would be the case for less developed regions.

## APPENDIX

### A MATHEMATICAL DERIVATION OF FIRST AND SECOND
### ORDER CONDITIONS OF UTILITY MAXIMIZATION

The Basic Model: Here, the objective is to maximize $U = U(C,P,S)$, where all first partials of $U$ are positive, all second partials are negative, and the cross-partial, $U_{cp}$, is positive. $U_{cs}$ and $U_{ps}$ are assumed to be zero. Maximization will be subject to the Constraint, $WT + Y = X(C,W) + J(P,W) + K(S,W)$.

First Order Conditions: Employing the Lagrangean method, we maximize:

$$N = U + \lambda (WT + Y - X - J - K)$$

...with respect to C, P, and S. Thus,

$$N_c = U_c - \lambda X_c = 0$$
$$N_p = U_p - \lambda^* J_p = 0$$
$$N_s = U_s - \lambda K_s = 0$$
$$N_\lambda = WT + Y - X - J - K = 0$$

...so that the usual condition that ratios of marginal utilities be equal to ratios of marginal expenses is obtained.

Second Order Conditions: Differentiating the first order conditions with respect to Wife's Real Wage (W), and Husband's and Other Family Income (Y), we obtain:

$$
\begin{bmatrix}
Ucc' & Ucp & 0 & -Xc \\
Ucp & Upp' & 0 & -Jp \\
0 & 0 & Uss' & -Ks \\
-Xc & -Jp & -Ks & 0
\end{bmatrix}
\begin{bmatrix}
\frac{\partial C}{\partial W} & \frac{\partial C}{\partial Y} \\
\frac{\partial P}{\partial W} & \frac{\partial P}{\partial Y} \\
\frac{\partial S}{\partial W} & \frac{\partial S}{\partial Y} \\
\frac{\partial \lambda}{\partial W} & \frac{\partial \lambda}{\partial Y}
\end{bmatrix}
=
\begin{bmatrix}
\lambda Xcw & 0 \\
\lambda Jpw & 0 \\
\lambda Ksw & 0 \\
T+L' & -1
\end{bmatrix}
$$

where $L'$ $(=(Xw+Jw+Kw))$ is the change in Wife's Labor Time, and $Ucc'$, $Upp'$, and $Uss'$ represent $(Ucc-\lambda Xcc)$, $(Upp-\lambda Jpp)$, and $(Uss-\lambda Kss)$ respectively. To insure that a maximum has in fact been achieved, the determinant of the Bordered Hessian must be negative (since there are three arguments in the Utility Function). Given the determinant, $D$, where:

$$D=Ks^2(Ucp^2-Ucc'Upp')-Uss'(Ucc'Jp^2-UcpXcJp+Upp'Xc^2)$$

...it will be sufficient if both of the following conditions hold:

(1) $Ucc'$, $Upp'$, and $Uss'$ are all negative. That is, the marginal utilities of C, P, and S must fall at a faster rate than the utility to be derived from any positive scale economies in the household production of the arguments.

(2) $Ucc'Upp'$ must be greater than $Ucp^2$. This is the standard rule of gross substitutes.

At this point, demand functions for C, P, and S with respect to changes in W and Y may be calculated (see text).

Integration of Socioeconomic Factors Into the Constraint: Urbanization: Expressing supplementary family
income from children as $m=m(C,R)$, where $m_c$ and $m_{RR}$ are
positive, and $m_R$, $m_{cc}$, and $m_{cR}$ are negative, the constraint
is rewritten as:

$$WT + Y = X + J + K - m$$

First order conditions are now:

$$Nc = Uc - \lambda(Xc - m_c) = 0$$
$$Np = Up - \lambda Jp = 0$$
$$Ns = Us - \lambda Ks = 0$$
$$N_\lambda = WT + Y + m - X - J - K = 0$$

Differentiating with respect to R, we obtain:

$$\begin{bmatrix} Ucc" & Ucp & 0 & (m_c - Xc) \\ Ucp & Upp & 0 & -Jp \\ 0 & 0 & Uss & -Ks \\ (m_c - Xc) & -Jp & -Ks & 0 \end{bmatrix} \begin{bmatrix} \frac{\partial C}{\partial R} \\ \frac{\partial F}{\partial R} \\ \frac{\partial S}{\partial R} \\ \frac{\partial \lambda}{\partial R} \end{bmatrix} = \begin{bmatrix} -\lambda m_{cR} \\ 0 \\ 0 \\ -m_R \end{bmatrix}$$

Second order conditions remain as above. $Ucc"$ is equal to
$Ucc - \lambda(Xcc - m_{cc})$.

Consumption Education: Here, the constraint is rewritten:

$$WT + Y = X(C,W,E) + J(P,W,E) + K(S,W,E)$$

Derivation of first and second order conditions are therefore the same as for changes in W (above), although $X_E$, $J_E$,
and $K_E$ are all negative.

# 5. AN ECONOMETRIC TEST

At the conclusion of Chapter 4, two sets of testable hypotheses are set down. First, there are those drawn from the direct effects (i.e., substitution, income, utility substitution) of various income and other socioeconomic factors on optimum family size; and second, hypotheses dealing with interactions relating the value per se of each independent variable to the magnitude of its own effect on fertility, as well as to the degree of influence other independent variables might have on optimum numbers of children. In this chapter, I construct and test an econometric model designed to examine the validity of these hypotheses.

While I admit the likelihood that a host of factors contribute to family planning, it is not my objective here to maximize the proportion of total variance on family size explained. Rather, I wish to construct a format whereby the role of each of husband's income (Y), wife's wage (W), parents' education (E), urbanization (R), grandparents' income (V), and fecundity time (T)[1] is more properly specified and understood in light of the theoretical model. Again, it should be pointed out that I am concerned about the long-run fertility behavior of the household, that is, the number of children parents expect to raise to maturity throughout the remainder of their child-bearing years.

Given the latter point, cross-sectional data are used. Ideally, such data should be drawn from areas that are stable

---

[1] Because of difficulties with the identification of an acceptable proxy, fecundity time is omitted from most tests.

from the standpoint of in- or out-migration. The reasoning
here stems from the fact that a high degree of mobility is
quite likely to be one of those factors which affect fertility
planning, but are outside the immediate scope of interest.
Should it be possible to control this factor, therefore, then
such control should be exercised.

In addition to those interactions suggested by the solution to the constrained welfare maximization problem, economic
theory strongly suggests that external paths of causality run
from some of the socioeconomic variables to others, i.e., education as investment in human capital, urbanization and its effects on family income, etc. Consequently, it is necessary to
begin by establishing a temporal framework designed to trace
these paths of causality, and to suggest rules by which various multicollinearities (causal or spurious) might be dealt with.
This task having been accomplished, the regression design may
be specified and tested. Finally, a set of preliminary conclusions about the various substitution and income effects men-
tioned can be deduced from coefficients obtained.

THE CAUSALITY SCHEME

As stated above, the numerous possibilities for multicollinearity among independent variables identified makes it im-
perative that some temporal framework be considered. This is
done for two reasons, the more immediate of which is, of course,
so that a means of treating the multicollinearity problem can
be devised. A second reason is a bit more long term in scope.

Specifically, while my interest here concentrates on the microeconomic question of how outside factors influence family size decisions, I should not wish to lose sight of the macroeconomic interdependence among income, socioeconomic, and fertility related variables. Thus, the causality scheme presented here, combined with conclusions drawn regarding the determinants of fertility behavior can be of future use in the development of models intended to predict growth paths of population and production through time.

The scheme I have decided upon is illustrated in Figure 5-1. Because urbanization has been increasing over the past several decades, and because fecundity time has two components, i.e., marriage age $(T_M)$ and divorce probability $(T_D)$, the scheme is

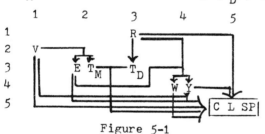

Figure 5-1

presented in two dimensions. To illustrate my rationale here, consider variables V, R, and E. From one perspective, it might be said that economic opportunities in urban areas gave rise to higher income levels for grandparents, enabling them to afford superior educational opportunities on behalf or parents. This is illustrated by the vertical dimension in which R is located at the earliest level of causality (1), and E at the latest (3). There is, however, an alternative perspective. Specifically,

more affluent grandparents give better educational opportunities to parents, who then migrate to urban areas. This is de-
picted by having horizontal movement in the scheme take us from
V to E, and only then to R. By way of procedure, I do not express preference for either 'dimension' of causality, and thus,
do not assume any definite priority in a temporal sense for R
as opposed to V or E, since between these pairs of variables,
conflicting orderings exist. Since V has priority over E in
both dimensions, however, a causal relationship is assumed there.

While the model presented in this chapter ends with the determination of optimum family size (C), the question of a simultaneous determination of the demands for child premium and
living standard (both represented collectively by 'SP' in Figure 5-1), as well as wife's labor supply (L) deserves some consideration. This is done in Chapter 6. Also, it should be noted that the system of causality just outlined is not closed.
Thus, W and Y influence the next generation of grandparents' income, a value that is also affected by C since a greater number
of children tend to lower the proportion of current family income saved. On the other hand, children may be able to contribute marginally to family income while they are still members
of their parents' household, or to stimulate by their existence
the productive propensities of parents. Thus, the foundation
for a population-production model is established.

A Theoretical Evaluation of Each Causality Path: The absence of interdimensional conflict in ordering is only a neces-

sary condition for the assumption of a causal relationship to be made. In addition, a degree of theoretical justification is required for a given path to be considered. Here, a summary of these justifications is offered so that a third set of hypotheses, i.e., those addressing external interrelationships among independent variables can be made.

(1) V and E: Since the educational achievement of parents depends to a great extent on grandparents' income, it is quite likely that some of the effect of V on C is contained within the coefficient of E. Thus, a possible correlation (positive) between V and E is considered causal in the sense that it is endogenous to the model. My method for treating this sort of relationship is presented below.

(2) V and Y: In that the general acceptability of working wives is a comparatively recent phenomenon, no causal relationship is expected to exist between V and W (although a statistical correlation might appear as the result of influences between V and E, and between E and W). There is, however, a twofold effect of V on Y. First, it is quite likely that a father who is successful at earning a substantial income will have accumulated a set of highly valuable contacts which may be passed onto his son. Thus, a positive correlation between V and Y is anticipated. Reenforcing the latter, moreover, is the effect on other family income (included in Y) which might occur as the result of any legacy accumulated by grandparents.

(3) V and $T_M$: Given the advisability of potential pa-

rents acquiring some minimum stock of wealth at the outset of marriage, I expect this minimum stock to be obtainable earlier should grandparents have the ability to provide financial assistance. Consequently, a negative relationship between V and $T_M$ is expected.

(4) E and W: Here, E can be considered a proxy for wife's education since the level of schooling for each parent is normally similar to that of the other. Given education as investment in human capital, therefore, a positive relationship between E and W is assumed.

(5) E and Y: The rationale here is the same as for the relationship between E and W just outlined.

(6) R and $T_D$: Since attitudes about divorce are somewhat more liberal (traditionally) in urban as opposed to rural areas, a path of causality reflecting an expected positive correlation is drawn from R to $T_D$.

(7) R and Y: An urban setting is probably conducive to a higher value of husband's income for several reasons. First, an urban environment provides more opportunities for those whose skills are highly specialized. Since such specialization generally commands a higher wage, it follows that a positive correlation between R and Y should exist. Secondly, since there are fewer opportunities for children to contribute to family income in an urban as opposed to a rural setting, a negative income effect is associated with urbanization. Thus, a higher value of Y would be one form of compensation. Finally, a wide

array of available consumer goods and services in the city suggests a positive 'utility income' effect for urbanization (see
Chapter 4). That is, I expect any wage rate at which the labor
supply curve bends backward to be higher in the city than in
the country.

(8) R and W: In addition to those reasons suggested to
support a causal and positive relationship between R and Y, I
expect the degree to which the idea of working wives is accepted in the city to be greater than it is in the country. Thus,
a positive correlation between R and W is expected.

Procedures for Dealing with Causality Paths: Having just
described the various sources of multicollinearity within an
econometric test of my model, one final task remains. That is,
it is necessary to develop a set of strategies for dealing with
(a) one-way causal relationships between pairs of independent
variables in the model, i.e., V and E, V and Y, R and W, R and
Y, E and W, E and Y, V and $T_M$, and R and $T_D$; and (b) correlations resulting either from the influences of exogenous factors
(perhaps V and R, or W and Y), or from a mutual dependence
(perhaps E and R) arising from a dimensional conflict in ordering within the causality scheme.

Whenever a path of causality exists between two independent variables in a given regression equation, then the dependent variable is made a function of the 'causing' factor, and
the residuals from the expected values of the 'effected' factor. Thus, coefficients may differ from those that would have

116

materialized had Ordinary Least Squares been used. This is because the contribution of covariance between the two independent variables is now attributed exclusively to the 'causing' factor, rather than evenly distributed between the latter and the 'affected' variable.[2]

For regressions containing independent variables that are either uncorrelated, or correlated in a way that is non-causal vis-a-vis the current framework, both independent variables appear in their original form, i.e., Ordinary Least Squares is used.

Finally, if two non-causally related independent variables produce regression coefficients that are equally significant to a degree that is less than statistically acceptable, then their individual employment may be replaced by an interaction variable derived from the product or quotient of the two original factors, provided that the coefficient of this compound term is statistically significant.

THE DATA

The Sample: As stated earlier, the long-run nature of the fertility planning problem in question suggests the use of a cross-sectional approach. In this vein, I have selected data from the 1970 Census of Population for approximately 200 counties each from three regions within the United States. The reason for using county data should be apparent. Here, I am able to obtain a wide degree of variance on each of the independent

[2]I assume, of course, that the relationships involved are linear.

variables in my model, as well as on the dependent variable.[3]
Moreover, the quantity of available data points is large enough
to eliminate those biases associated with small samples, while
still permitting sufficient control over any cultural variables
not included in the model. By way of disadvantage, however, I
find that an adequate proxy for age of marriage is absent at
the county level. Consequently, the fecundity time factor is
not used in my regressions.

The three regions selected include the Midwest (Iowa, Kansas, and Nebraska), the Northeast (New York, Ohio, and Pennsylvania), and the Southeast (Alabama and Georgia). The rationale
for selecting these states and regions should be made clear.
Specifically, I am interested in interactions among those factors affecting fertility behavior, as well as in the specific
effects of each variable per se. Recalling the second set of
hypotheses made at the conclusion of Chapter 4, and the general
expectation implied by these hypotheses, i.e., that economic development tends to reduce impacts of the independent variables
I am using to test fertility behavior, it follows that the use
of several regions of differing degrees of economic development
is more instructive than would be the case were a single region
used. As illustrated below, the three regions selected did represent (at least until 1970) different degrees of economic development.

Given the importance of agriculture, and the presence of

[3]While longitudinal data would have offered a degree of variance greater than that with county data, that which is currently available does not offer data on grandparents' income.

older, industrial cities in many of the states selected, I must
be concerned about the possibility of significant intrastate
migration; the recent technological revolution in agriculture
having rendered many farm families redundant, while the general
trend toward suburbanization having caused many urban families
to move into suburbs often in different counties. To minimize
this difficulty, I eliminated all counties for which fewer than
seventy percent of households living in the county in 1970 were
residents of the same county in 1965 (1970 Census of Population,
Table 119). Here, I operate under the assumption, verified by
much of the literature on migration, that areas of heavy in-migration are also subject to heavy out-migration.

Below, I show that as proxies for wife's wage and husband's
income, it is possible to use income of families with a female
head, and a function of median family income respectively.
Since a small sample increases the possibility that a given income distribution may be unacceptably skewed, thus creating a
greater disparity between mean and median; I have eliminated
from my sample all counties with fewer than one hundred female
headed households. Finally, some of the counties have populations too small to permit the recording of some data. Therefore, all counties with fewer than 3000 persons were also eliminated.

The use of county data does have some additional shortcomings. First, there is the possibility that rural behavior is
overrepresented relative to the size of rural population since

the ratio of rural to urban counties exceeds the ratio of rural to urban residents. Second, as implied by the reference to husband's income, above, less than perfect proxies must sometimes be used. Finally, there is no acceptable proxy for fecundity time at the county level. Thus, that variable had to be eliminated from these tests.[4]

The Variables: To begin, I have selected proxies for Numbers of Children (the dependent variable), Wife's Wage, Urbani-

Table 5-1

THE VARIABLES

| VARIABLE | PROXY | REFERENCE |
|---|---|---|
| Number of Children (C) | Number of Children Ever Born Per 100 Females Over 25 Years of Age | Table 120 |
| Wife's Wage (W) | Mean Income of Females Who Were Family Heads in 1969 (100's of dollars) | Table 124 |
| Urbanization (R) | Proportion of County Population Living in Urban Areas (tenths of percentage points) | Table 9 |
| Grandparents' Income (V) | Median Family Income in 1960 (100's of dollars) | Table 121 (City-County Data Book-1962) |
| Parents' Education (E) | Median Years of Schooling for Males Over 25 Years of Age (tenths of years) | Table 120 |
| Family Income (Y') | Median Family Income in 1970 (100's of dollars) | Table 124 |
| Wife's Labor Force Participation (L) | Ratio of Married Women in the Labor Force to Number of Married Women (Husband Present) | Table 121 |

[4]Using the proportion of 15-19 year olds who were family heads or wives of family heads to represent T(M), and the ratio of divorced to married females for T(D), coefficients obtained led to a strong suspicion that variances on fecundity time are attributable to cultural factors not included in the model, but capable of affecting family size in a way that is contrary to that of T, and strong enough to create unacceptable distortions in the observed correlation between fecundity time and fertility.

zation, Parents' Education, Grandparents' Income, Family Income, and Wife's Labor Force Participation, the latter two factors being combined with Wife's Wage to create a proxy for Husband's Income. These are identified in Table 5-1 (additional notes on data are provided in the Chapter 6 Appendix).

As stated above, several of these proxies have imperfections. Specifically:

(1) It must be assumed that the distribution of wages earned by females who are family heads is the same as that for employed married women, husband present (proxy for W).

(2) It must be assumed that a strong negative correlation exists between the proportion of county residents living in urban centers, and the proportion of county population living on farms (proxy for R).

(3) It must be assumed that migration patterns from 1960-1965 did not differ substantially from those from 1965-1970 (proxy for V).

(4) As suggested earlier, a strong positive correlation must be assumed to exist between median education of males and median education of females (proxy for E).

(5) The assumption made with respect to the proxy for W is also required in order to proceed with the calculation of a proxy for Y.

Husband's Income: Since no acceptable proxy for Husband's Income is offered at the county level, it is necessary for one to be manufactured. Recognizing that family income is affected

by both of wife's wage and her labor force participation, the
first step is to regress Median Family Income on the product
WL. The results of these regressions are recorded in Table
5-2. Standard errors are in parentheses.

Table 5-2

Y' = Y'(WL), COEFFICIENTS

|  | MIDWEST | NORTHEAST | SOUTHEAST |
|---|---|---|---|
|  | Y'=47.57+.015WL (.001) | Y'=50.48+.018WL (.0014) | Y'=33.75+.016WL (.001) |
| $R^2$ | .440 | .510 | .432 |
| F | 155.77 | 214.37 | 148.02 |

I believe that an acceptable proxy for Y can now be calculated by merely subtracting the effect of WL from Y'. Thus,
values for husband's income are found using (Y'-.015WL) for
the Midwestern counties, and (Y'-.018WL) and (Y'-.016WL) for
the Northeast and Southeast respectively

THE REGRESSIONS

Regressions at Earlier Stages of Causality: Having identified possible paths of external causality, and having set
down procedures by which these paths might be incorporated into
the model, I now determine the extent to which suspected correlations actually exist. First, a summary of this third set
of hypotheses is offered in Table 5-3.

Table 5-3

EXPECTED COEFFICIENT SIGNS

|  |  | AFFECTED VARIABLE | | |
|---|---|---|---|---|
|  |  | E | W | H |
| AFFECTING VARIABLES | V | positive | --- | positive |
|  | R | --- | positive | positive |
|  | E | --- | positive | positive |

Given the third set of hypotheses, the next step is to
perform regressions for which E and W are dependent variables.
Results here are presented in Table 5-4.  Again, standard errors are in parentheses.

Table 5-4

FACTORS AFFECTING E AND W
(COEFFICIENTS)

$E = E(V)$

| MIDWEST | NORTHEAST | SOUTHEAST |
|---|---|---|
| .530(.058)* | .557(.044)* | .903(.054)* |
| Constant: 93.840 | 85.934 | 63.860 |
| $R^2$   .294 | .437 | .589 |
| F   82.44 | 157.76 | 279.07 |

$W = W(R,E)$

| | MIDWEST | NORTHEAST | SOUTHEAST |
|---|---|---|---|
| R | .006(.003)+ | .012(.002)* | .0003(.0029) |
| E | .083(.102) | .538(.090)* | .336(.061)* |
| Constant: | 44.682 | - 5.386 | 11.404 |
| $R^2$ | .035 | .341 | .164 |
| F | 3.567 | 52.300 | 10.100 |

* Sig. at 1%  + Sig. at 5%  o Sig. at 10%

By way of general comment, it can be seen that all coefficient signs are consistent with experimental hypotheses, although a wide range of statistical significance does appear.
Of greater interest, I believe, is the fact that E and R are
able to explain a considerably greater proportion of the total
variance on W in the Northeast than for the other regions.
This is quite probably a demand-oriented phenomenon, suggesting that labor markets are more 'institutionalized' in the
Northeast, being concentrated to a great extent in urban cen-

ters, and being less likely to extend opportunities to less educated females.

Having explored those paths of causality leading to parents' education and wife's wage, all that remains is to examine husband's income as a function of V, R, and the residuals
of E given V (i.e., Er). Results of regressions designed to do
this are presented in table 5-5.

Table 5-5

FACTORS AFFECTING Y
(COEFFICIENTS)

|  | MIDWEST | NORTHEAST | SOUTHEAST |
|---|---|---|---|
| V | .585(.082)* | .804(.081)* | .916(.056)* |
| R | .000(.003) | -.0015(.0027) | -.010(.002)* |
| Er | .092(.072) | -.136(.095) | .566(.068)* |
| Constant: | 22.26 | 7.78 | 8.41 |
| $R^2$ | .365 | .494 | .662 |
| F | 37.57 | 55.34 | 93.93 |
| Er = E - | (93.840+.530V) | (85.934+.557V) | (63.860+.903V) |

* Sig. at 1%      + Sig. at 5%      o Sig. at 10%

While the coefficients of V are positive (as expected),
and highly significant for all three regions, some surprises
occur with R and Er coefficients. In the case of urbanization,
coefficients are either insignificant, or, in the case of the
Southeast, significant but negative! I suspect that reasons
for the latter anomaly lie with the fact that (a) several highly urbanized counties in the Southeast were excluded from my
sample because of heavy in-migration during the 1960's, and (b)
unlike other regions, where organized labor is comparatively
stronger in the urban than in rural areas, it has not pro-

gressed to a great extent in either environment in the Southeast,[5] an observation that can also be of use in accounting for
the significantly positive impact of education on husband's
earnings in the Southeast, in contrast to the other two regions.
Specifically, a robust union movement could succeed in narrow-
ing the income differential between 'more educated' and 'less
educated' occupations, especially during a period of national
prosperity as existed at least until 1970. Since such a movement was less apparent in the Southeast, the effect of education
on earning power there remained largely intact.

The Demand for Numbers of Children: Having accounted for
paths of causality among variables determined to affect fertility behavior, I may now proceed to regress family size (C)
on all of V, R, Er, Wr, and Yr, where Wr and Yr are respective
residuals from expected values of wife's wage and husband's income. Before presenting my findings here, note should be taken of a modification within the Midwest regression. Specifically, in the initial regression for that region[6], urbanization
and grandparents' income coefficients were negative, as expected, but statistically insignificant. Recall that in such an
event, I propose the use of an interaction term consisting of
the product or quotient of the factors in question. Here, the

---

[5]See: U.S. Dept. of Labor, Bureau of Labor Statistics, HAND-
BOOK OF LABOR STATISTICS, Bulletin 2070, Dec., 1980.

[6]i.e., C = 384.500 + 1.0261Yr + 0.6977Wr - 0.0170R - 1.693Er
                 (.4512)     (.2901)      (.0141)     (.3952)
           - 0.7536V
             (.4952)     $R^2$ = .175    F = 8.26

fact that both coefficients are of the same sign leads me to
employ the product, RV. It is this final specification, then,
the results of which appear, along with those of Southeast and
Northeast regressions in Table 5-6.

Table 5-6
$$C = C(V,R,Er,Wr,Yr)$$
(COEFFICIENTS)

|  | MIDWEST | NORTHEAST | SOUTHEAST |
|---|---|---|---|
| V | --- | -.006(.397) | -4.049(.473)* |
| R | --- | -.061(.012)* | .024(.016) |
| RV | -.00066(.00017)* | --- | --- |
| Er | -1.734(.394)* | .259(.427) | -2.197(.556)* |
| Wr | .645(.269)+ | .259(.328) | -1.892(.542)* |
| Yr | 1.022(.449)+ | .369(.326) | - .497(.581) |
| Constant | 357.158 | 353.890 | 620.763 |
| $R^2$ | .176 | .266 | .482 |
| F | 10.39 | 14.42 | 35.59 |

* Sig. at 1%    + Sig. at 5%    o Sig. at 10%

The regressions having been performed, findings may now be
examined from the perspective of the two sets of hypotheses
summarized at the close of Chapter 4. I begin with the first
set, i.e., hypotheses dealing with substitution, income, and
utility substitution effects of individual independent variables.

With respect to grandparents' income (V), I expect an inverse relationship with planned fertility, the utility substitution effect of higher accustomed levels of consumption suggesting a slower rate of decline in Uss for parents. This relationship is clearly its strongest in the Southeast (t =-8.56).
While some semblance of the negative utility substitution effect here is indicated in the Midwest, its strength relies on,

and varies directly with urbanization. Meanwhile, V seems to have no effect on fertility behavior in the Northeast.

In addition to a negative utility substitution effect, the urbanization variable (R) is also incorporated into the constraint of the welfare maximization problem, where increases in its value are shown to generate negative substitution and income effects which are more traditional. Despite their reenforcing nature, all three of these effects within $\partial C/\partial R$ are weak in the Midwest and Southeast. For both regions, tests using V and R seperately (see Footnote 6) produce coefficients for R that fall short of statistical significance, although urbanization does have an impact in the Midwest by virtue of its interaction with V. Note that such an RV interaction term is not used in the Southeast or Northeast, since V and R respectively were able to provide significant coefficients by themselves in those regions.

In retrospect, the failure of urbanization to prove significant to fertility behavior in the Midwest and Southeast is not surprising. In the first place, differences in the array of available consumer goods, the principal cause of the utility substitution effect here, are probably not so great in a developed as opposed to a less developed economic entity. Secondly, it would seem that the material value of children as sources of income in the United States is less than for a society where productive activity is more labor intensive. Thus, those substitution and income effects associated with the impact of a change in R on full family wealth are similarly small.

While consistent with a priori expectations, the highly significant, negative urbanization coefficient in the Northeast regression is an enigma in light of observations stated above vis-a-vis the corresponding coefficient in the Midwest and Southeast regressions. By way of speculation, it is possible that, despite the point made above dealing with urban-rural differences in the array of consumer goods between LDC's and MDC's, the utility substitution effect from changes in R is significant in the Northeast. This is because that region, with its substantially greater concentration of large metropolitan areas, offers a greater variance on the mean value of urbanization.[7] Consequently, urban-rural contrasts are more apparent in the Northeast than in either the Midwest or Southeast.

In contrast to the Southeast and Midwest, where highly significant, negative education coefficients suggest a decided dominance of the substitution over the income effect from changes in that independent variable, the corresponding coefficient for the Northeast is positive, but insignificant. Apparently, then, the positive income and negative substitution effects arising from changes in parents' education are offsetting in the Northeast, i.e., the 'technological' effect of education on household production functions is factor neutral. This point is explored further in the discussion of interactions among independent variables below.

The negative substitution effect resulting from a change

[7]Variances on mean R for the Midwest, Northeast, and Southeast respectively are 62,557, 66,897, and 56,476. See the Appendix to Chapter 6.

in wife's wage appears to be, relative to the positive income effect, quite formidable. This contrasts quite sharply with results from the other regions. In the Northeast, for example, these effects appear, given the insignificant coefficient, to be offsetting; while in the Midwest, a significant, positive coefficient suggests a dominant income effect. This point as well is relevant to the discussion of interactions below.

Finally, it is hypothesized that increases in husband's income would have a positive effect on the demand for numbers of children. Such a relationship only materialized, however, in the Midwest, coefficients of Y being insignificant elsewhere.

Having examined regression results in the context of my first set of hypotheses, I can now give consideration to those hypotheses dealing with interactions among independent variables. To develop a perspective on interregional levels of the latter, mean values of C, Y', R, E, L, and V are presented in Table 5-7. Clearly, the fact that the Southeast had (1970) the

Table 5-7
MEAN VALUES

|     | MIDWEST    | NORTHEAST  | SOUTHEAST  |
|-----|------------|------------|------------|
| C   | 345        | 326        | 358        |
| Y'  | $7800      | $9200      | $6300      |
| R   | .385       | .461       | .297       |
| E   | 11.7 yrs.  | 11.6 yrs.  | 9.1 yrs.   |
| L   | 36%        | 37%        | 43%        |
| V   | $4400      | $5400      | $3000      |

lowest mean values of income variables (Y' and V) indicates a

relatively modest degree of economic development for that region. Its low mean values for urbanization and parents' education, moreover, serve to reenforce this conclusion, these variables generally increasing with development as well.

With respect to the general expectation that income and
socioeconomic variables play a greater role in optimum fertility in less developed societies or regions, my findings seem to
offer a good deal of support, $R^2$ being considerably higher in
the Southeast than in the other regions. For more specific hypotheses, the regression results presented here suggest:

(1) A reduction in the marginal utility of income does seem
to diminish as well those traditional substitution effects associated with changes in wife's wage and parents' education. Observe that coefficients for both of these independent variables
are strongly negative in the Southeast. In the Midwest, in
contrast, the education coefficient is negative, but that of
wife's wage is positive (both are significant); while in the
Northeast, neither coefficient is significant. Moreover, since
I expect this decline in importance in the substitution effect
given increased levels of economic development to apply to
changes in urbanization as well, I am further convinced that the
significantly negative coefficient of that factor in the Northeast is attributable to the utility substitution effect.

(2) A lower rate of decline in the marginal utility of income is anticipated to reduce the expected positive values of
income effects, while the result of increased urbanization on

the rate of decline in the marginal income potential of children (i.e., $m_{cc}$--see Chapter 4) is believed to raise these income effects. Using coefficients for husband's income as an indicator of which of these forces is the stronger, results here are inconclusive. Specifically, the more highly urbanized Midwest provides a significant and positive Y coefficient, in contrast to the less urbanized Southeast, where that coefficient is insignificant. Thus, for the range of R values represented by those regions, the $m_{cc}$ interaction appears to be greater in magnitude than the Uss interaction. For the range of R between the Midwest and the Northeast, however, the opposite appears to be the case, the coefficient of husband's income for the latter region being insignificant.

## 6. TOWARD THE SIMULTANEOUS ESTIMATION OF THE DEMANDS FOR NUMBERS OF CHILDREN AND ALTERNATIVES TO CHILDREN, AND WIFE'S LABOR SUPPLY

Given efforts by Cain & Dooley and by Fleisher & Rhodes to determine simultaneous estimates of such items as family size, the demands for child quality and living standard, and wife's labor force participation (see Chapter 3), I believe it useful to expand my original econometric model in a way that is similar. The main reason for doing this is to provide some helpful insights into the consistency of coefficients obtained for regressions presented in Chapter 5. Given the assumed time intensity of child rearing, for example, my theoretical model suggests that if the negative substitution effect within $\partial C/\partial W$ is of a lesser magnitude than the positive income effect, then a higher value of wife's wage would serve to reduce her labor supply since a greater amount of her time is now being used for household production. Now, if wife's wage coefficients were positive (as with Midwestern counties in the regressions presented in Chapter 5), added confidence can be developed in these positive signs by showing here that the coefficient of wife's wage is negative in regressions for wife's labor supply. By the same token, I am interested in the effect of changes in W on the demand for alternatives to children. If indeed $\partial C/\partial W$ is positive, and if child rearing is time intensive, then regressions designed to test the demand for child premium and/or living standard should have coefficients for wife's wage that are positive, and hopefully, more significant than their counterparts in regressions for numbers of children.

By way of agenda, I examine first the demand for alternatives to children following the same theoretical and econometric principles used earlier with the demand for numbers of children. Here, I use housing demand to represent those alternatives since housing contains aspects of both child premium and living standard, and because the production of housing services is probably less time intensive than child rearing.

The discussion of housing demand is followed by an examination of wife's labor force participation, again using those techniques set down in Chapters 4 and 5. Having thus developed a set of independent regressions for numbers of children, alternatives to children, and wife's labor supply, the stage is set for the simultaneous estimation of all three of the latter. This is done by regressing each of the three dependent variables in question on the residuals of the other two, in addition to those socioeconomic and income variables used previously. Again, seperate regressions are performed for Midwestern, Northeastern, and Southeastern counties.

HOUSING DEMAND AND WIFE'S LABOR SUPPLY, INDEPENDENT ESTIMATES

Housing Demand and the Theoretical Framework: To begin, I reconsider the problem of constrained welfare maximization as presented originally in Chapter 4. Recalling that this is a Becker-type model, it might be of use to restate some of the principal assumptions with which I am working. First, each of the three arguments of the utility function requires inputs of both market goods and wife's time in order to be 'produced'.

Secondly, the three production functions are of a nature such that, given the employment of optimum input combinations, the production of child services is time intensive relative to that of either premium or living standard. That is, an increase in wife's wage has a greater impact on the marginal cost of children than it has on the marginal costs of alternatives. Thirdly, various socioeconomic factors (i.e., grandparents' income, urbanization, parents' education, and fecundity time) have a potential influence on (a) the household production functions and/or (b) the structure of the utility function. Finally, these socioeconomic variables influence each other as well as income variables in such a way as to necessitate the formulation of an appropriate causality scheme. Having restated these points, I proceed to regress the demand for housing services on those socioeconomic and income variables with which I have been working, along with a proxy representing the market price of housing services. Comment on coefficients is reserved for later when the final simultaneous estimates are made.

The Data: Housing demand as a proxy for child premium and living standard is represented by rooms per household member; specifically, the ratio of Median Rooms (All Occupied Units) to Median Number of Persons per Occupied Unit. The source is the 1970 Census of Housing. Data on the price of housing services are also obtained from this source. Here, I employ as a proxy Median Contact Rent for Dwellings With Complete Plumbing Facilities, divided by Median Rooms per Unit. All other data are as described in Chapter 5 (see Appendix).

As with other values extracted at the county level, the proxy for housing does have some shortcomings. Specifically, I am obliged to assume the absence of any significant variance in square footage per housing unit (for which data are not available) among counties with similar values for median rooms per occupied unit. Also, the use of 'occupied units' omits the contribution of 'vacation cottages' or 'summer homes' to housing services, so I must assume that the latter are of trivial importance. Nevertheless, this could create a downward bias vis-a-vis the positive income effect on housing demand given changes in W or Y.

Procedures: By way of procedure, the first step is to determine the relationship between housing supply, as represented by urbanization (an inverse proxy), and housing price. I can then proceed to examine the demand for housing as a function of grandparents' income, urbanization, parents' education, wife's wage, husband's income, and of course, the price of housing services. The resulting regression equation can then be called on below, along with similar regressions for fertility behavior and wife's labor supply, in the construction of a more complete model of household behavior.

The Findings: Results of regressions designed to test the influence of urbanization on the price of housing services are presented in Table 6-1. Here, price is denoted by 'K'.

While the significantly positive coefficients obtained

Table 6-1
K AS A FUNCTION OF R

|  | MIDWEST | NORTHEAST | SOUTHEAST |
|---|---|---|---|
|  | .067(.005) | .106(.009) | .029(.006) |
| Constant: | 66.85 | 63.93 | 69.93 |
| $R^2$ | .492 | .426 | .095 |

All coefficients are significant at 1%

here for all three regions are consistent with expectations, the relatively lower degree of explanatory power of R in the Southeast reflects, as in tests described in Chapter 5, the effect of my having excluded several of the more urbanized counties of that region.

Using 'Kr' to denote residuals from regression results reported above, housing demand, SP, can now be regressed itself on V, R, Er, Wr, Yr, and Kr. Results are given in Table 6-2. Er, Wr, and Yr are as in Chapter 5.

Table 6-2
$$SP = SP(V,R,Er,Wr,Yr,Kr)$$
COEFFICIENTS

|  | MIDWEST | NORTHEAST | SOUTHEAST |
|---|---|---|---|
| V | -.502(.185)* | .011(.191) | .338(.143)+ |
| R | -.037(.005)* | -.016(.006)* | .005(.004) |
| Er | .551(.125)* | .799(.177)* | .346(.153)+ |
| Wr | .106(.090) | .081(.149) | -.256(.150)o |
| Yr | .272(.145)o | -.725(.145)* | -.528(.147)* |
| Kr | -.423(.060)* | -.243(.033)* | -.171(.054)* |
| Constant: | 224.900 | 163.330 | 140.090 |
| $R^2$ | .650 | .500 | .287 |
| F | 60.04 | 32.98 | 12.73 |

\* Sig. at 1%    + Sig. at 5%    o Sig. at 10%

While a more detailed set of comments on housing demand regression coefficients is reserved for the more complete model of simultaneous estimates presented below, a few superficial observations come to mind here. First, as expected, the coefficient of Kr is negative and significant for all regions. Secondly, each of the three education coefficients is positive, not an unexpected result for the Midwest and Southeast in light of the education-fertility relationships reported for those regions in Chapter 5; while coefficients of urbanization are negative, suggesting a greater role for that factor in housing supply as opposed to housing demand. Again, I discount the insignificant R coefficient in the Southeast regression by virtue of the exclusion of counties having experienced heavy in-migration during the 1960's.

Wife's Labor Force Participation: Since wife's labor supply is that amount of her time available after consideration has been taken of required time inputs for household production, I can write:

$$L^* = T - t_c(W)C^* - t_p(W)P^* - t_s(W)S^*$$

...where the 't' functions each represent optimum per unit time inputs given wife's wage, and $C^*$, $P^*$, and $S^*$ are optimum demands for numbers of children, child premium, and living standard given those socioeconomic and income factors incorporated into my model. Since T is total available time, then, I note that optimum labor supply, $L^*$, is itself a function of V, R, Er, Wr, and Yr. It is with the effects of these variables, then, that I am concerned here. Recognizing, however, that various

religious or other cultural factors can create positive or
negative deviations from expected values of C and SP, it is
clear that these residuals also contribute to the determination of wife's labor market activity. Thus, the rationale for
the more complete set of simultaneous estimates presented below
is apparent. As with housing demand, then, I begin by regressing L independently on V, R, Er, Wr, and Yr. For the three
regions being used here, this latter set of tests produced results summarized in Table 6-3.

Table 6-3
L = L(V,R,Er,Wr,Yr)
COEFFICIENTS

|  | MIDWEST | NORTHEAST | SOUTHEAST |
|---|---|---|---|
| V | .227(.048)* | .330(.049)* | -.068(.056) |
| R | .005(.001)* | -.0044(.0015)* | .012(.002)* |
| Er | .182(.039)* | .097(.049)+ | -.358(.066)* |
| Wr | -.070(.027)+ | -.134(.040)* | .071(.065) |
| Yr | -.230(.043)* | -.586(.039)* | -.563(.069)* |
| Constant: | 13.350 | 16.702 | 48.569 |
| $R^2$ | .485 | .618 | .455 |
| F | 36.66 | 64.25 | 31.87 |

\* Sig. at 1%  + Sig. at 5%  o Sig. at 10%

Again, comment on these results is postponed until the ex-
position of the complete model of simultaneous estimates, below. Suffice to say here, the negative coefficients of Yr are
consistent with theoretical expectations, as well as with econometric investigations done previously by others. Similarly,
coefficients of wife's wage are in agreement with those determined in the independent examination of fertility (Chapter 5).

With respect to other independent variables, anomalies occur with coefficient signs of Er in the Southeast, R in the Northeast, and perhaps, V in both the Midwest and Northeast.

THE COMPLETE MODEL

Having formulated a complete set of independent estimates for C, SP, and L for each of the Midwestern, Northeastern, and Southeastern regions, I move now to the task of developing simultaneous equations describing the demands for numbers of children and housing services, and wife's labor supply.

Theoretical Considerations: Fertility and Housing Demand:

While housing is used here to represent alternatives to numbers of children, it nevertheless has a role to play in all three of the household production functions. With respect to the production of child services, it appears likely that some minimum input of housing is essential for the support of a specific number of children. Given this minimum, therefore, parents may feel that the quality of children can be improved through additional inputs of housing, i.e., seperate bedrooms for children, playrooms, etc. In other words, housing can also be used as an input in the production of child premium. Finally, housing can be employed to further the living standard of parents, i.e., in-home studies, summer homes, etc. In the econometric tests presented here, housing is represented by the ratio of median rooms per dwelling to median persons per dwelling. Consequently, the sign of the fertility coefficient with respect to housing is expected to be either zero or negative for

three reasons. First, I expect scale economies to be present
so far as minimum housing needed to support children is concerned. Secondly, even if I were able to remove from my calcu-
lations of housing those rooms for general use, i.e., kitchen,
dining and living rooms, baths, etc., required even by childless
households, the ratio of rooms to occupants would fall with the
births of children unless additional rooms were added for each
child. While it is possible that this increment of housing
could be exceeded (i.e., a seperate bedroom and bath for each
child), this would quite likely be offset so far as the ratio
of rooms to family members is concerned by the existence within parents' quarters of additional rooms that are not subsequently converted for use by children. Finally, an increase in
family size will, given the constraint of the utility maximization problem, leave less resources (i.e., goods and time) available for living standard. Since the latter might also be improved through better housing, therefore, I conclude that the
demand for housing services falls with increases in family size.

Housing, Fertility, and Wife's Labor Supply: Having specified wife's labor supply as the residual remaining after the
temporal inputs required for optimum levels of household production have been deducted from total available time, I simplify
the expression set down earlier to read:

$$L^* = T - t_c(W)C^* - t_s(W)SP^*$$

...where SP* here represents optimum levels of alternatives to
children in general.

Next, three classes of derivatives are identified:

(a) For changes in C (or SP) resulting from exogenous cultural factors:

$$\partial L/\partial C = -t_c(W) - t_s(W)(\partial SP/\partial C)$$

Here, wife's labor force participation varies inversely with number of children, provided that $-t_c(W)$ is the dominant factor on the right side. Given that SP here includes child premium as well as living standard, and given the relative time intensity of child rearing, this is probably the rule rather than the exception.[1]

(b) Given changes in endogenous factors not directly affecting household technology, husband's income for example:

$$\partial L/\partial Y = -t_c(W)(\partial C/\partial Y) - t_s(W)(\partial SP/\partial Y)$$

Since the derivatives of C and SP with respect to Y are both expected to be positive, there is no ambiguity in the expected sign of $\partial L/\partial Y$. Note that this need not be the case given changes in V or R, where traditional and utility substitution effects may cause C and SP to move in opposite directions. Again, however, the time intensity of child rearing and the inclusion of both premium and living standard within SP suggest that the first term on the right is dominant.

(c) Finally, if a variable that does influence household technology, i.e., W, should change, then:

$$\partial L/\partial W = -t_c'(W)C - t_c(W)(\partial C/\partial W) - t_s'(W)SP - t_s(W)(\partial SP/\partial W)$$

Since $t_c'(W)$ and $t_s'(W)$ are expected to be negative, it follows that an upward sloping supply curve for wife's labor requires

---

[1] Although in the short run, this might not be true, especially for women with older children.

the production substitution effects plus the normal substitution effect within $\partial C/\partial W$ together to outweigh the combined income effects plus the normal substitution effect within $\partial SP/\partial W$.

The Estimates: Given the hypothesis that optimum values
of C, SP, and L are determined simultaneously, the completed
set of estimates for each of the Midwestern, Northeastern, and
Southeastern regions is presented in Table 6-4-A, B, and C.
Observe that the residuals Cr, SPr, and Lr are derived from the
independent estimates made above and in Chapter 5. Coefficients
derived using Ordinary Least Squares are also provided so that
the influence of my causality specification can be determined.

Observations: An initial observation is that the addition
of Cr, SPr, and Lr in regressions for C, SP, and L has minimal
effect on other coefficients when compared to independent regressions (Chapter 5, Table 5-6; Chapter 6, Tables 6-2 & 6-3).
Thus, while the introduction of variables representing values
codetermined with the dependent variable in each regression
makes it possible to account for a greater proportion of variance, the influence is that the omission of these codetermined
values leads to a minimum of bias.

Secondly, the substantial increase from the addition of
SPr and Lr in an already high $R^2$ value for the Southeast fertility regression appears to lend additional support to the general hypothesis that socioeconomic and income factors play a
greater role in determining optimum family size in less as opposed to more developed regions. Of lesser significance here,

Table VI-4A

C = C(V,R,Er,Wr,Yr,SPr,Lr)

COEFFICIENTS

|  | MIDWEST | NORTHEAST | SOUTHEAST |
|---|---|---|---|
| V | --- | -.008(.384) | -4.049(.353)* |
| R | --- | -.061(.012)* | .025(.012)+ |
| RV | -.00065(.00015)* | --- | --- |
| Er | -1.450(.336)* | .266(.386) | -2.221(.414)* |
| Wr | .657(.234)* | .270(.314) | -1.908(.404)* |
| Yr | .869(.368)* | .320(.305) | - .512(.433) |
| SPr | -1.223(.192)* | -.584(.158)* | -2.717(.226)* |
| Lr | -.871(.617) | .563(.575) | -1.319(.451)* |
| Constant | 737.916 | 416.086 | 1064.466 |
| $R^2$ | .321 | .313 | .716 |
| F | 15.29 | 12.84 | 67.96 |

C = C(V,R,E,W,Y,SP,L)

COEFFICIENTS

|  | MIDWEST | NORTHEAST | SOUTHEAST |
|---|---|---|---|
| V | -.779(.628) | -.565(.765) | -.562(.686) |
| R | -.028(.015)o | -.063(.011)* | .042(.014)* |
| E | -.969(.409)+ | .121(.391) | .220(.477) |
| W | .589(.261)+ | .264(.324) | -2.936(.440)* |
| Y | .526(.421) | .421(.453) | -3.013(.557)* |
| SP | -.548(.188)* | -.042(.143) | -2.432(.233)* |
| L | -1.439(.676)+ | .210(.578) | -1.489(.479)* |
| Constant | 619.712 | 334.499 | 1050.695 |
| $R^2$ | .214 | .267 | .681 |
| F | 7.53 | 10.23 | 57.65 |

*Sig. at 1%    +Sig. at 5%    oSig. at 10%

Table VI-4B

$$SP = SP(V,R,Er,Wr,Yr,Kr,Cr,Lr)$$

COEFFICIENTS

|  | MIDWEST | NORTHEAST | SOUTHEAST |
|---|---|---|---|
| V | -.170(.175) | .159(.183) | .482(.107)* |
| R | -.044(.005)* | -.020(.005)* | .001(.002) |
| Er | .614(.111)* | .797(.167)* | .478(.114)* |
| Wr | .177(.081)+ | .162(.142) | -.124(.112) |
| Yr | .415(.131)* | -.652(.138)* | -.440(.110)* |
| Kr | -.641(.064)* | -.310(.035)* | -.265(.041)* |
| Cr | -.173(.024)* | -.138(.033)* | -.166(.013)* |
| Lr | .347(.226) | .802(.244)* | -.158(.109) |
| Constant | 293.518 | 193.871 | 246.233 |
| $R^2$ | .728 | .561 | .612 |
| F | 64.18 | 31.25 | 37.04 |

$$SP = SP(V,R,E,W,Y,K,C,L)$$

COEFFICIENTS

|  | MIDWEST | NORTHEAST | SOUTHEAST |
|---|---|---|---|
| V | -.806(.183)* | -.662(.369)+ | .030(.168) |
| R | -.009(.004)+ | .002(.006) | .010(.003)* |
| E | .148(.128) | .798(.182)* | .528(.116)* |
| W | .329(.087)* | .104(.168) | -.638(.114)* |
| Y | .699(.152)* | -.331(.229) | -.796(.136)* |
| K | -.657(.065)* | -.304(.096)* | -.236(.085)* |
| C | -.179(.024)* | -.020(.035) | -.142(.014)* |
| L | .365(.227)+ | .859(.284)* | -.188(.119)o |
| Constant | 297.808 | 152.090 | 244.373 |
| $R^2$ | .731 | .408 | .541 |
| F | 65.36 | 16.92 | 27.67 |

*Sig. at 1%    +Sig. at 5%    oSig. at 10%

Table VI-4C
L = L(V,R,Er,Wr,Yr,Cr,SPr)
COEFFICIENTS

| | MIDWEST | NORTHEAST | SOUTHEAST |
|---|---|---|---|
| V | .223(.048)* | .329(.048)* | -.066(.055) |
| R | .005(.001)* | -.0044(.0015)* | .012(.002)* |
| Er | .185(.039)* | .096(.048)+ | -.358(.065)* |
| Wr | -.069(.027)+ | -.134(.039)* | .070(.063) |
| Yr | -.231(.042)* | -.586(.038)* | -.563(.068)* |
| Cr | -.012(.008) | .008(.009) | -.033(.011)* |
| SPr | .002(.024) | .062(.020)* | -.077(.047)o |
| Constant | 18.477 | 3.959 | 79.960 |
| $R^2$ | .492 | .635 | .479 |
| F | 26.70 | 49.02 | 24.87 |

L = L(V,R,E,W,Y,C,SP)
COEFFICIENTS

| | MIDWEST | NORTHEAST | SOUTHEAST |
|---|---|---|---|
| V | .172(.065)+ | .727(.079)* | .446(.097)* |
| R | .0042(.0015)* | -.0028(.0015)o | .007(.002)* |
| E | .212(.041)* | .127(.047)* | -.052(.071) |
| W | -.060(.028)+ | -.122(.039)* | -.030(.072) |
| Y | -.210(.042)* | -.529(.041)* | -.635(.076)* |
| C | -.016(.007)+ | .003(.009) | -.033(.011)* |
| SP | -.049(.020)+ | .041(.017)+ | -.079(.043)o |
| Constant | 32.039 | 8.572 | 79.701 |
| $R^2$ | .505 | .622 | .482 |
| F | 28.135 | 46.33 | 25.10 |

*Sig. at 1%    +Sig. at 5%    oSig. at 10%

but consistent with this observation is that $R^2$ for the Midwest, while lower than that for the Northeast in independent regressions of C, is raised to parity with the latter when Lr and SPr are included.[2]

In Chapter 4, I hypothesize that economic development tends to reduce the marginal utility of income, and thus, substitution effects from changes in R, E, and W. Empirical evidence presented in Chapter 5 tends to support this hypothesis. In examining findings here, however, I find that while support for the development-substitution effect relationship is maintained, and perhaps enhanced, some doubt arises with respect to the cause. Specifically, I suspect that the weakening of substitution effects here may also be caused by a general tendency toward equalization of factor proportions in household production. In retrospect, this seems logical since the higher value of W in a more developed region causes less time intensive techniques of child rearing to be used by parents. Thus, while the latter activity is still time intensive relative to alternatives to children, the degree to which it is so is reduced. Also, development itself can provide, through improvements in household technology, the means by which less time intensive techniques can be made available. Thus, while the general increase in algebraic values of coefficients of Er and Wr (i.e., those factors whose effects are not clouded by utility substitution or supply effects) can be attributed to a decline in the marginal

---

[2]While I recognize that higher $R^2$ values frequently result from higher variances on dependent and/or independent variables, such is not the case here, see Appendix.

utility of income, this latter explanation is also worthy of consideration. Now, upon examination of coefficients for co-determined variables within C, SP, and L regressions, an interesting pattern emerges. Specifically, in all cases (i.e., $\partial C/\partial SPr$, $\partial C/\partial Lr$, $\partial SP/\partial Lr$, and their reciprocals) coefficients tend to grow in algebraic value as the state of development rises. In several cases this movement also carries a loss in 't' value as well, and as such, can be associated with the declining importance of substitution effects. With respect to $\partial SP/\partial Lr$ and $\partial L/\partial SPr$, however, coefficients are negative and insignificant in the Southeast, but positive and significant in the Northeast! Since the impact on family size of changes in variables to which substitution effects are attributed remain of lesser algebraic value than influences on housing demand, I conclude that substitution effects, while reduced, do not disappear altogether. Thus, the effect of development on $\partial SP/\partial Lr$ and its reciprocal must be attributed to some degree to improved technology in the area of home maintenance, and that some portion of the decline in significance of coefficients for $\partial C/\partial Er$ and $\partial C/\partial Wr$ is the consequence of a positive relationship between development and the technology of child rearing. With respect to the original set of independent variables, not much need be said here about regressions testing family size, no significant changes having occured from the incorporation of SPr and Lr. Concerning the demand for housing and wife's labor supply, coefficient signs tend to be as anticipated, and although some deviations do occur, they seem to be rather isolated. Taking these variables in turn, I note:

(1) Status, as represented by grandparents' income, appears to influence housing demand to a significant degree only in the Southeast, V coefficients being positive and negative, but insignificant, for the Northeast and Midwest respectively. Conversely, status is a positive factor in wife's labor supply in the latter regions, but not in the Southeast. An interaction with interregional differences in the time intensity of home maintenance as discussed above is suspected here.

(2) Urbanization appears, with the possible exception of the Southeast, to be more of a supply than a demand factor in regressions for SP. While increases in R do seem, as expected, to encourage greater labor force participation on the part of married women, the Northeast results do present a significant anomaly here.

(3) Parents' Education coefficients are consistent with expectations if the proposition that improved household technology occurs with economic development is accepted. Specifically, Er coefficients are all positive in SP regressions, and are positive for the Midwest and Northeast regressions for L. Thus, the strong negative Er coefficient in the Southeast labor supply regression is an appropriate response to the greater household demands on wife's time implied by the positive $\partial SP/\partial Er$ coefficient for that region.

(4) Although some of the 't' values of Wr coefficients in

L and SP regressions are low, the signs of these coefficients
are consistent with expectations given the observed effects of
changes in wife's wage on the demand for numbers of children.

(5) While the significantly negative coefficients of Yr
in all three regressions for wife's labor supply are quite in
line with expectations, negative coefficients for that variable in SP regressions for the Northeast and Southeast are a
puzzle. Unless omitted variables have created a bias by being
correlated positively with Yr and negatively with SP, the only
explanation would be that, once those housing requirements
needed for status (as represented by V) are met, housing then
becomes an inferior good vis-a-vis increases in husband's income.

(6) The negative and significant coefficients of Er in all
SP regressions are fully consistent with theoretically derived
hypotheses.

A final set of observations deals with estimates obtained
using Ordinary Least Squares as opposed to my own method of
'covariance allocation' via a causality scheme. Table 6-5 sum-
marizes the effect of OLS on 't' values, (+) and (-) signs de-
noting increases to statistical significance and reductions from
significance respectively. While no definite pattern emerges
here, it does appear that those factors placed at earlier levels
in the causality scheme (i.e., R, V, and possibly Er) are the
most likely to have coefficient 't' values that are sensitive
to method of specification, especially in regressions designed

Table 6-5

EFFECT OF OLS ON 't' VALUES

DEPENDENT VARIABLE

| INDEP. VAR. | C Region | | | SP Region | | | L Region | | |
|---|---|---|---|---|---|---|---|---|---|
| | MW | NE | SE | MW | NE | SE | MW | NE | SE |
| V |  |  | − | + | + | − |  |  | + |
| R | + |  |  |  | − | + |  |  |  |
| E |  | − |  | − |  |  |  |  | − |
| W |  |  |  |  |  | + |  |  |  |
| Y | − | + |  |  | − |  |  |  |  |
| P |  | − |  |  |  |  | + |  |  |
| C |  |  |  |  |  |  | + |  |  |
| L |  |  |  |  |  |  |  |  |  |

to test housing demand. While these distortions occur less frequently in regressions for numbers of children and wife's labor supply, there are serious implications where it does take place (observe the differences in $\partial C/\partial V$ and $\partial C/\partial E$ for the Southeast). Moreover, since the direction of any distortion depends on covariances among independent variables, it may be quite difficult to predict.

APPENDIX

## Summary of Data

| VARIABLE | SOURCE | MEAN/VARIANCE |
|---|---|---|
| Numbers of Children (C) | Number of Children Ever Born Per 100 Females Over 25 Years of Age. Census of Population (1970), Table 120 | MW 345/1318<br>NE 326/966<br>SE 358/3141 |
| Housing Demand (SP) | Median Rooms, All Occupied Units divided by Median Persons Per Occupied Unit. Census of Housing (1970) Tables 61 & 62. % points. | MW 230/280<br>NE 205/198<br>SE 172/203 |
| Wife's Labor Supply (L) | Ratio of Married Women (Husband Present) in the Labor Force to Total Married Women. Census of Population (1970, Table 124. % points | MW 36/23<br>NE 37/28<br>SE 43/42 |
| Grandparents' Income (V) | Median Family Income in 1960. City-County Data Book--1962, Table 121. $100's. | MW 44/60<br>NE 54/71<br>SE 30/72 |
| Urbanization (R) | Proportion of County Population Living in Urban Areas. Census of Population (1970), Table 9. 1/10's of % points. | MW 385/62557<br>NE 461/66897<br>SE 297/56476 |
| Parents' Education (E) | Median Years of Schooling for Males over 25 Years of Age, Census of Population (1970), Table 120. 1/10's of years | MW 117/58<br>NE 116/50<br>SE 91/99 |
| Wife's Wage (W) | Mean Income of Families With Female Head in 1969. Census of Population (1970), Table 124. $100's | MW 58/80<br>NE 62/107<br>SE 42/80 |
| Family Income (Y') | Median Family Income in 1970. Census of Population (1970, Table 124. $100's | MW 78/112<br>NE 92/192<br>SE 63/154 |
| Housing Cost (K) | Median Contact Rent for Dwellings With Complete Plumbing Facilities, divided by Median Rooms Per Unit. Census of Housing (1970), Tables 61 & 62. $ per Room | MW 64/159<br>NE 74/200<br>SE 46/59 |

# 7. GENERAL SUMMARY AND CONCLUSIONS

As stated at the beginning of Chapter 1, my objective is to develop a testable model examining the economic determinants of human fertility behavior, building upon those foundations established by Becker, and refined by Willis, DeTray, Michael, and others. I believe there is much to be gained from a clearer understanding of choice given scarce resources in the area of fertility behavior, the long-run allocation of educational expenditures, the anticipation of future demands for the services of public and private insurance programs, and the evaluation of capital projects whose usefullness and/or costs are a function of population growth, to provide just a few examples.

Although the 'intuituve' approach identified with Easterlin has been quite fruitful, I have chosen to follow Becker's method of family welfare maximization given constraints of household technology because it is more conducive to the identification of numerous 'effects' from changes in any of the set of income or socioeconomic factors included in the model. Since many of these effects are quite subtle, they are not always likely to be appreciated using intuition alone.

My procedure has been to develop the model theoretically (Chapter 4); to construct an independent econometric test of the model confining the set of independent variables to grandparents' income, urbanization, parents' education, wife's wage, and husband's income (Chapter 5); and finally, to develop a more complete model for the simultaneous estimation of the demands for numbers of children and alternatives to children, and wife's labor force participation (Chapter 6).

General Summary: The theoretical model is quite standard from the Becker perspective, beginning with a utility function whose arguments are numbers of children, child premium, and living standard. These 'commodities' are in turn 'produced' according to, and maximum total utility constrained by, a set of household production functions, inputs of which are market goods and wife's time. It is assumed that child rearing is time intensive relative to the production of child premium and living standard.

Drawing on the works of DeTray, Michael, and others, the next step involves the integration of various socioeconomic factors into the fabric of the constrained welfare maximization problem, where income variables were introduced previously. The solution to the problem is then shown to contain (a) standard substitution and income effects given variations in wife's wage and husband's income, as well as in urbanization, parents' education, and fecundity time in their effects on production technology, additional family income, or the duration of the household's lifespan, (b) utility supstitution effects given changes in grandparents' income or urbanization, and (c) risk effects resulting from parents' risk minimization preferences, and the ways in which changes in income, education, and urbanization might affect the costs of realizing these preferences.

Initial tests of the model appear in Chapter 5. Here, data from some 200 Midwestern, Northeastern, and Southeastern counties are used to observe the degree to which numbers of children desired is affected by variations in grandparents' income, urbanization, parents' education, husband's income, and wife's wage. Recognizing the many sources of multicollinearity, however, it was considered necessary to construct a temporal framework, or causality scheme, before the actual regressions were performed. Here, two dimensions of causality are identified using those directions of influence suggested by economic theory as being most likely.

A complete model recognizing that decisions governing the demand for numbers of children, the demand for alternatives to children, and the supply of wife's labor are made simultaneously is tested in Chapter 6. Here, housing services are called on to represent both child premium and living standard, i.e., alternatives to children. Among the results obtained were:

(1) Income and socioeconomic variables have a profound impact on fertility behavior in the least economically developed region (the Southeast), explaining over seventy percent of the variance on C, in contrast to the more developed Midwest (32%), and the most developed Northeast (31%). These same factors, on the other hand, account for over sixty percent of the variance in wife's labor force participation in the Northeast, where I suspect economic development has led to more institutionalized labor markets. Meanwhile, $R^2$ values for L regressions are about 49% and 48% for the Midwest and Southeast respectively. Finally, the ability of independent variables employed to ac-

count for variance in housing demand follows no clear pattern vis-a-vis development, $R^2$ values ranging from 56% (Northeast) to about 73% (Midwest).

(2) Patterns of coefficient signs and 't' values appear to indicate a reduction in the magnitudes of substitution effects as development progresses. Here, I focus attention on coefficients of parents' education and wife's wage. For both variables, I observe highly significant and negative correlations in fertility regressions for the Southeast, the same but to a slightly reduced extent for the Midwest, and virtually no significance in the Northeast.

(3) While Er and Wr coefficients in housing demand and wife's labor supply regressions are somewhat consistent with observation (2), above, some deviation does occur, i.e., a negative Er coefficient in the Southeast labor supply regression. I suspect, however, that much of the anomaly here can be attributed to income effects created by the influence of development on household technology, an observation that gains credibility upon examination of coefficient patterns of Cr, SPr, and Lr, i.e., the general tendency for algebraic values of these coefficients to rise with development.

(4) For all regions, an increase in husband's income tends to reduce wife's labor force participation. Using implied increases in the availability of both goods and time resulting from higher values of Yr as a standard for observing the strength of income effects, I note a clear pattern, positive Yr coeffi-

cients in the Northeast and Midwest regressions indicating some propensity for allocating greater full income to numbers of children, while negative coefficients in Southeast regressions for both C and SP suggesting a general tendency away from domestic activity as family income grows.

(5) With respect to utility substitution effects, my findings seem to indicate that, except for Midwest fertility and wife's labor supply regressions, either V or R can assume a major role in behavior, but not both. Examples here include (a) the dominating negative effects on fertility of urbanization in the Northeast, and grandparents' income in the Southeast,[1] (b) the negative influences of urbanization on housing demand in the Midwest and Northeast, in contrast to the strongly positive effect of grandparents' income in the corresponding regression for the Southeast, and (c) a large and positive 'V' coefficient of wife's labor supply in the Northeast, as opposed to a similarly large and positive urbanization coefficient in that regression using data from the Southeast.

Suggestions for Further Research: As is usually the case when one attempts to tie off some of the loose ends currently

[1] The marginal impact of V on fertility in the Midwest combined with the considerable effect of that variable on family size in the Southeast seems to support Easterlin's expectations regarding status and expected consumption. While Olneck & Wolfe (1978) have misgivings here, their data is taken from a large city (Detroit), and as such, are consistent with my own findings using data from the urbanized Northeast. Thus, it appears that the 'Easterlin Hypothesis' becomes less valid as economic development progresses.

existing in a given area of study, a multitude of new questions arises. Such is the case here, a number of general areas for further examination immediately presenting themselves.

First, with the many differences I have found to exist in fertility behavior among three regions of the United States, it might be interesting to determine the extent to which such differences occur among different countries per se, different regions of the world, and among different societies at, as with the Southeast, Midwest, and Northeast, various stages of economic development. While many of those following the Easterlin method (i.e., Adelman, Friedlander & Silver, etc., see Chapter 2) have made noteworthy contributions here, little in this area has come from econometric specifications using Becker's concepts as a theoretical basis. If, for example, the Northeast did indeed represent a more advanced stage of economic development in 1970 than did the Midwest or Southeast, then one might speculate that the weakening of the negative correlation between desired number of children and socioeconomic factors progresses as a general rule. Alternatively, however, urbanization, as Michael might contend (see Chapter 3), could serve as an alternative to education so far as the distribution and acceptance of contraceptive information and techniques are concerned.

Secondly, in addition to the value of my model as a tool for predicting future trends in family size, female labor force participation, etc., I believe it to have considerable worth as a basis whereby our understanding of household behavior can be further refined. Specifically, I would expect to derive valuable insights into those factors affecting such behavior, but not included in the model as presented here. This is to be done by gathering data of both a quantitative and qualitative nature from those counties having significant deviations from expected values of C, L, or SP. Should patterns emerge indicating a relevance for such factors theoretically capable of generating the kinds of substitution, income, and/or utility substitution effects outlined here, then such factors could be integrated into the framework of the theoretical model and its econometric specification. Along these same lines, there is much to be learned from studies that focus in greater depth on specific independent variables affecting fertility behavior, especially those of a socioeconomic nature. Here, one might also include interactions between certain cultural factors and these variables. It might be asked, for example, why it is that among more conservative Catholics, Mormons, various Amish sects, etc., where large families are the rule, those factors identified here as exerting a negative influence on fertility may or may not be depended on to temper such cultural and religious tradition. Alternatively, we might wish to know if higher fertility rates among non-whites as opposed to whites is attributable exclusively to differences in their distribution vis-a-vis income and socioeconomic factors, or explained, at least in part, by purely cultural characteristics.

Thirdly, to what degree can variables found to influence

158

fertility in a positive way serve to offset the less than average fertility of such less traditional but increasingly wide-
spread types of households as those headed by educated, working mothers with husband not present?

Finally, it may be of interest to combine our efforts here
with those of Kuznets, Simon, Coale & Hoover, et al discussed
earlier (Chapter 2) in order to develop a growth model in which
both production and population growth are codependent. While
this would bring us full circle back to Malthus, much would
have been learned in the process.

## BIBLIOGRAPHY

Adelman, Irma. 1963. "An Econometric Analysis of Population Growth". AMERICAN ECONOMIC REVIEW 53: 314-319

Adelman, Irma & Cynthia Taft Morris. 1966. "A Quantitative Study of Social and Political Determinants of Fertility". ECONOMIC DEVELOPMENT AND CULTURAL CHANGE 14: 129-157.

Becker, Gary S. 1960. "An Economic Analysis of Fertility". In DEMOGRAPHY AND ECONOMIC CHANGE IN DEVELOPED COUNTRIES. Princeton, N.J.: Princeton University Press, for the National Bureau of Economic Research.

————. 1965. "A Theory of the Allocation of Time". ECONOMIC JOURNAL 75(299): 493-517.

————. 1973. "A Theory of Marriage: Part I". JOURNAL OF POLITICAL ECONOMY 81(4): 813-846.

————. 1974. "A Theory of Marriage: Part II". JOURNAL OF POLITICAL ECONOMY 82(2, pt 2): S11-S26.

————. 1981. A TREATISE ON THE FAMILY. Cambridge, Mass.: Harvard University Press.

Blake, Judith. 1966. "Ideal Family Size Among White Americans: A Quarter Century's Evidence". DEMOGRAPHY 3: 154-73.

————. 1968. "Are Babies Consumer Durables?" POPULATION STUDIES 22: 5-27.

Blandy, Richard. 1974. "The Welfare Analysis of Fertility Reduction". THE ECONOMIC JOURNAL 84: 109-129.

Butz, William P. and Michael P. Ward. 1979. "Will U.S. Fertility Remain Low? A New Interpretation". POPULATION AND DEVELOPMENT REVIEW 5(4): 563-588.

Bumpass, L. 1969. "Age of Marriage as a Variable in Socio-Economic Differentials in Fertility". DEMOGRAPHY 6: 45-54.

Cain, Glen & Martin Dooley. 1976. "Estimation of a Model of Labor Supply, Fertility, and Wages of Married Women". JOURNAL OF POLITICAL ECONOMY 84(3): 179-201.

Coale, Ansley J. 1960. "Population Change and Demand, Prices, and the Level of Employment". In DEMOGRAPHIC AND ECONOMIC CHANGE IN DEVELOPED COUNTRIES. Ansley Coale, ed. Princeton: Princeton University Press

Coale, Ansley & Edgar M. Hoover. 1958. POPULATION GROWTH AND ECONOMIC DEVELOPMENT IN LOW-INCOME COUNTRIES. Princeton: Princeton University Press.

Coale, Ansley & Melvin Zelnick. 1963. NEW ESTIMATES OF POPULATION AND FERTILITY IN THE UNITED STATES. Princeton: Princeton University Press.

Demeny, Paul. 1979. "On the End of the Population Explosion". POPULATION AND DEVELOPMENT REVIEW 5(1): 141-162.

160

DeTray, Dennis N. 1973. "Child Quality and the Demand for Children". JOURNAL OF POLITICAL ECONOMY 81(2 pt. 2): S70-S95.

_____. 1978. "Child Schooling and Family Size: An Economic Analysis". R-2301-NICHD. Santa Monica, Calif.: RAND.

Easterlin, Richard A. 1961. "The American Baby Boom in Historical Perspective". AMERICAN ECONOMIC REVIEW 51: 869-911.

_____. 1967. "Effects of Population Growth on the Development of Developing Countries". THE ANNALS OF THE AMERICAN ACADEMY OF POLITICAL AND SOCIAL SCIENCE 369: 98-108.

_____. 1968. POPULATION, LABOR FORCE, AND LONG SWINGS IN ECONOMIC GROWTH. New York: NBER.

_____. 1969. "Towards a Socio-Economic Theory of Fertility: Survey of Recent Research on Economic Factors in American Fertility". In FERTILITY AND FAMILY PLANNING: A WORLD VIEW, S.J.Behrman, Leslie Corsa, and Ronald Freedman, eds. Ann Arbor: University of Michigan Press.

Enke, Stephen, et al. 1970. ECONOMIC BENEFITS OF SLOWING POPULATION GROWTH. Santa Barbra: Tempe.

Espenshade, Thomas J. 1977. "The Value and Cost of Children". POPULATION BULLETIN 32(1). Washington, D.C.: Population Reference Bureau.

Fleisher, Belton M. & G.F. Rhodes, Jr. 1979. "Fertility, Women's Wage Rates, and Labor Supply". AMERICAN ECONOMIC REVIEW 69: 14-25.

Freedman, Deborah. 1963. "The Relation of Economic Status to Fertility". AMERICAN ECONOMIC REVIEW 53: 414-26.

Freedman, Ronald & Lolagene Coombs. 1966. "Child Spacing and Family Economic Position". AMERICAN SOCIOLOGICAL REVIEW 31: 631-48.

Friedlander, Stanley & Morris Silver. 1967. "A Quantitative Study of the Determinants of Fertility Behavior". DEMOGRAPHY 4: 30-70.

Gardner, Bruce. 1973. "Economics of the Size of North Carolina Rural Families". JOURNAL OF POLITICAL ECONOMY 81(2, pt. 2): S99-S122.

Ghez, Gilbert R. & Bary S. Becker. 1975. THE ALLOCATION OF TIME AND GOODS OVER THE LIFE CYCLE. New York: Columbia University Press, for the NBER.

Gregory, Paul R. 1973. "Differences in Fertility Determinants: Developed and Developing Countries". THE JOURNAL OF DEVELOPMENT STUDIES 9: 233-41.

Grossman, Michael. 1971. "The Economics of Joint Production in the Household". Report 7145. Center for Mathematical Studies in Business and Economics, University of Chicago.

Hansen, Alvin H. 1939. "Economic Progress and Declining Population Growth", AMERICAN ECONOMIC REVIEW 29: 1-15.

Hawthorn, Geoffrey. 1970. THE SOCIOLOGY OF FERTILITY. London: Collier-,acMillan.

Heckman, James J. 1976. "A Life-Cycle Model of Earnings, Learning, and Consumption." JOURNAL OF POLITICAL ECONOMY 84(2, pt. 2): S11-S44.

Heer, David M. 1966. "Economic Development and Fertility". DEMOGRAPHY 3: 423-444.

Henderson, James M & Richard E. Quandt. 1980. MICROECONOMIC THEORY: A MATHEMATICAL APPROACH. New York: McGraw-Hill.

Hirshleifer, Jack. 1955. "The Exchange Between Quantity and Quality". QUARTERLY JOURNAL OF ECONOMICS 69(4): 596-606.

Hoover, Edgar M. 1969. "Economic Consequences of Population Growth". INDIAN JOURNAL OF ECONOMICS 196: 101-111.

Houthakker, H.S. 1952. "Compensated Changes in Quantities and Qualities Consumed". REVIEW OF ECONOMIC STUDIES 19(3): 155-64.

Ishikawa, Tsuneo. 1975. "Family Structures and Family Values in the Theory of Income Distribution". JOURNAL OF POLITICAL ECONOMY 83(5): 987-1008.

Iyoha, Milton Ame. 1973. "Human Fertility, Population Change, and Economic Development". Econometric Society Paper. Dec.

Jaffe, A.J. 1940. "Differential Fertility in the White Population in Early America". JOURNAL OF HEREDITY 31(9): 407-11.

Kasarda, John D. 1971. "Economic Structure and Fertility: A Comparative Analysis". DEMOGRAPHY 8: 307-18.

Kirk, Dudley. 1969. "Natality in the Developing Countries: Recent Trends and Prospects". In FERTILITY AND FAMILY PLANNING: A WORLD VIEW. S.J.Behrman, Leslie Corsa, and R. Freedman, eds. Ann Arbor: University of Michigan Press.

Kuznets, Simon. 1958. "Long Swings in the Growth of Population and in Related Economic Variables". PROCEEDINGS OF THE AMERICAN PHILOSOPHICAL SOCIETY 102: 25-52.

_____. 1960. "Population Change and Aggregate Output". In DEMOGRAPHIC AND ECONOMIC CHANGE IN DEVELOPED COUNTRIES. Princeton: Princeton University Press.

_____. 1973. POPULATION, CAPITAL, AND GROWTH. New York: Norton.

_____. 1974. "Rural-Urban Differences in Fertility: An International Comparison. PROCEEDINGS OF THE AMERICAN PHILOSOPHICAL SOCIETY 118: 1-29.

Kuznets, Simon et al. 1957-64. POPULATION, REDISTRIBUTION, AND ECONOMIC GROWTH, UNITED STATES 1870-1950. 3 vols. Philadelphia: University of Pennsylvania Press.

Landes, William M. & Solomon, Lewis C. 1972. "Compulsory Schooling Legislation: An Economic Analysis of Law and Social Change in the Nineteenth Century". JOURNAL OF ECONOMIC HISTORY 32(1): 54-91.

Laslett, Peter, ed. 1972. HOUSEHOLD AND FAMILY IN PAST TIME. London: Cambridge University Press.

Lebergott, Stanley. 1960. "Population Change and the Supply of Labor". In DEMOGRAPHIC AND ECONOMIC CHANGE IN DEVELOPED COUNTRIES. A.J. Coale, ed. Princeton: Princeton University Press.

Leibenstein, Harvey. 1954. A THEORY OF ECONOMIC DEMOGRAPHIC DEVELOPMENT. Princeton: Princeton University Press.

_____, 1957. ECONOMIC BACKWARDNESS AND ECONOMIC GROWTH. New York: Wiley.

_____, 1972. "The Impact of Population Growth on the American Economy". In THE REPORT OF THE COMMISSIONS ON POPULATION GROWTH AND THE AMERICAN FUTURE. Vol. 2: ECONOMIC ASPECTS OF POPULATION CHANGE.

MaCurdy,T.E. 1981. "An Empirical Model of Labor Supply in a Life-Cycle Setting". JOURNAL OF POLITICAL ECONOMY 89(4): 1059-1080.

Malthus, Thomas R. 1798. AN ESSAY ON THE PRINCIPLE OF POPU-LATION, AS IT AFFECTS THE FUTURE IMPROVEMENTS OF SOCIETY. London: J.Johnson.

Michael, Robert. 1971. "Dimensions of Household Fertility: An Economic Analysis". American Statistics Association Annual Meeting, Social Statistics Section: 126-36.

_____. 1973. "Education and the Derived Demand for Children". JOURNAL OF POLITICAL ECONOMY 81, (pt 2 of 2), S128-64.

Michael, Robert T. & Robert J. Willis. 1973. "Contraception and Fertility: Household Production Under Uncertainty". Working Paper No. 21. Center for Economic Analysis of Human Behavior and Social Institutions, New York, December.

Mincer, Jacob & Walter Polachek. 1974. "Family Investments in Human Capital: Earnings of Women". JOURNAL OF POLITICAL ECONOMY 82 (pt 2 of 2): S56-93.

Myrdal, Gunnar. 1940. POPULATION: A PROBLEM FOR DEMOCRACY. Cambridge: Harvard University Press.

Namboodiri, N. Krishnan. 1970. "Economic Status and Family
Size Preference". POPULATION STUDIES 24: 235-37.

_____. 1972. "Some Observations on the Economic Framework
for Fertility Analysis". POPULATION STUDIES 26: 185-206.

Okun, Bernard. 1958. "Trends in Birth Rates in the United
States Since 1870". Baltimore: Johns Hopkins University
Press.

Olneck, M.R. & B.L.Wolfe. 1978. "A Note on Some Evidence on
the Easterlin Hypothesis". JOURNAL OF POLITICAL ECONOMY
86(4): 953-57.

Perlman, Mark. 1981. "Population and Economic Change in Developing Countries: A Review Article". JOURNAL OF ECONOMIC
LITERATURE 19: 78-92.

Phillips, Llad, & Harold L. Votey,Jr. 1969. "A Synthesis of
the Economic and Demographic Models of Fertility: An Econometric Test". REVIEW OF ECONOMICS AND STATISTICS 51:
298-308.

Pitchford, J.D. 1974. POPULATION IN ECONOMIC GROWTH. Am-
sterdam: North Holland.

Pollak, Robert & Michael L. Wachter. 1975. "The Relevance
of the Household Production Function and its Implications
for the Allocation of Time." JOURNAL OF POLITICAL ECONOMY
83(2): 255-77.

Preston, Samuel H. 1972. "Marital Fertility and Female Employment Opportunity: United States, 1960." Mimeo. De-
partment of Demography, University of California,
Berkeley.

Preston, Samuel H. & Alan T. Richards. 1975. "The Influence
of Women's Work Opportunities on Marriage Rates". DEMO-
GRAPHY 12(2): 209-222.

Rainwater, Lee. 1965. FAMILY DESIGN: MARITAL SEXUALITY,
FAMILY SIZE, AND CONTRACEPTION. Chicago: Aldine.

Rosen, Sherwin. 1978. "Substitution and Division of Labour".
ECONOMICA 45(179): 235-50.

Rosenzweig, Mark R. & Kenneth I. Wolpin. 1980a. "Life-Cycle
Labor Supply and Fertility: Causal Inferences from Household Models". JOURNAL OF POLITICAL ECONOMY 88(2): 328-354.

_____. 1980b. "Testing the Quantity-Quality Fertility Model:
The Use of Twins as a Natural Experiment". ECONOMETRICA
48(1): 227-240.

Ruggles, Richard & Nancy Ruggles. 1960. "Differential Fer-
tility in the United States". In DEMOGRAPHIC AND ECONOMIC
CHANGE IN DEVELOPED COUNTRIES. A. Coale, ed. Princeton:
Princeton University Press.

Ryder, Norman B. 1969. "The Emergence of a Modern Fertility Pattern: United States 1917-66. In FERTILITY AND FAMILY PLANNING: A WORLD VIEW. S.J.Behrman, Leslie Corsa, and R. Freedman, eds. Ann Arbor: University of Michigan Press.

Samuelson, Paul A. 1956. "Social Indifference Curves". QUARTERLY JOURNAL OF ECONOMICS 70(1): 1-22.

Sanderson, Warren & Robert J. Willis. 1971. "Economic Models of Fertility: Some Examples and Implications". NBER Annual Report: 32-42.

Sattinger, Michael. 1975. "Comparative Advantage and the Distribution of Earnings and Abilities". ECONOMETRICA 43(3): 455-68.

Schorr, Alvin. 1965/1970. "Income Maintenance and the Birth Rate". SOCIAL SECURITY BULLETIN 27: 22-30.

Schultz, T. Paul. 1969a. "An Economic Perspective of Population Growth". Mimeo.

_____. 1969b. "An Economic Model of Family Planning and Fertility". JOURNAL OF POLITICAL ECONOMY 77: 153-80.

Schultz, T.W. 1963. THE ECONOMIC VALUE OF EDUCATION. New York: Columbia University Press.

Scrimshaw, Susan C.M. 1978. "Infant Mortality and Behavior in the Regulation of Family Size". POPULATION AND DEVELOPMENT REVIEW 4(3): 383-403.

Seiver, Daniel A. 1974. "An Empirical Study of Declining Fertility in the United States" PhD. Yale University.

Silver, Morris. 1965. "Births, Marriages, and Business Cycles in the United States". JOURNAL OF POLITICAL ECONOMY 73: 237-55.

Simon, Julian. 1974. "The Effects of Income on Fertility". Monograph 19. Chapel Hill, N.C.: Carolina Population Center, University of North Carolina.

_____. 1977. THE ECONOMICS OF POPULATION GROWTH. Princeton: Princeton University Press.

Simon, Rita James & Julian L. Simon. 1974/1975. "The Effect of Money Incentives on Family Size: A Hypothetical-Question Study". PUBLIC OPINION QUARTERLY (Winter): 585-95.

Spengler, Joseph J. 1952. "Population Theory". In A SURVEY OF CONTEMPORARY ECONOMICS, Vol. 2. B. Haley, ed. Homewood: Irwin.

_____. 1964. "Population and Economic Growth". In POPULATION: THE VITAL REVOLUTION, R. Freedman, ed. New York: Doubleday Anchor.

_____. 1966. "The Economist and the Population Question". AMERICAN ECONOMIC REVIEW 56: 1-24.

_____. 1966. "Values and Fertility Analysis". DEMOGRAPHY 3: 109-130.

Stys, W. 1957. "The Influence of Economic Conditions on the Fertility of Peasant Women". POPULATION STUDIES 11: 136-48.

Sweezy, Alan. 1971. "The Economic Explanation of Fertility Changes in the United States". POPULATION STUDIES 25: 255-267.

Sweet, James A. 1974. "Differentials in the Rate of Fertility Decline: 1960-1970". FAMILY PLANNING PERSPECTIVES 6(2): 103-107.

Tarver, J.D. 1956. "Costs of Rearing and Educating Farm Children". JOURNAL OF FARM ECONOMICS 28: 144-153.

Thirlwall, Anthony P. 1972. "A Cross Section Study of Population Growth and the Growth of Output and Per Capita Income in a Production Possibilities Framework". MANCHESTER SCHOOL OF ECONOMICS AND SOCIAL SCIENCES 40: 339-56.

Tomes, Nigel. 1978. "A Model of Child Endowments, and the Quality and Quantity of Children". PhD. University of Chicago.

U.S. Bureau of the Census. 1973a. CENSUS OF HOUSING. Washington, D.C.: Government Printing Office.

_____. 1973b. CENSUS OF POPULATION. Washington, D.C.: Government Printing Office.

Weintraub, Robert. 1962. "The Birth Rate and Economic Development". ECONOMETRICA 40: 812-17.

Westoff, Charles & Norman Ryder. 1969. "Recent Trends in Attitudes Toward Fertility Control and in the Practice of Contraception in the United States". In FERTILITY AND FAMILY PLANNING: A WORLD VIEW. S.J.Behrman, Leslie Corsa, and R. Freedman, eds. Ann Arbor: University of Michigan Press.

Whelpton, P.K. & C.V.Kiser, eds. 1946/1950/1952/1954/1958. SOCIAL AND PSYCHOLOGICAL FACTORS AFFECTING FERTILITY. Vols. 1-5. New York: Milbank Memorial Fund.

Williams, Anne D. 1979. "Fertility Determinants in the United States: A Test of the Relative Income Hypothesis". Unpublished memorandum. University of Pennsylvania.

Willis, Robert J. 1973. "A New Approach to the Economic Theory of Fertility Behavior". JOURNAL OF POLITICAL ECONOMY 81(2, pt. 2): S14-S64.

Yasuba, Yasukichi. 1962. BIRTH RATES OF THE WHITE POPULATION IN THE UNITED STATES, 1800-1860: AN ECONOMIC STUDY. Baltimore: Johns Hopkins University Press.

Yaukey, David. 1961. FERTILITY DIFFERENCES IN A MODERNIZING COUNTRY. Princeton: Princeton University Press.

Zaidan, George C. 1969. "Population Growth and Economic Development". STUDIES IN FAMILY PLANNING 42. Population Council of New York. May.

Zitter, Meyer. 1970. "Population Trends in Metropolitan Areas". AMERICAN STATISTICAL ASSOCIATION PROCEEDINGS, SOCIAL STATISTICS SECTION.